beyond DRES

Personal Stylists' Secrets to Confidence

Margaret Spencer, DRES System Founder

with Personal Stylists

Lisa Fischer

Giselle Royston

Mary Angelosante

Lori Goddard-Weed

Wendy Petersen

ISBN: 978-0-9965796-0-5

Cover and page design by Margaret Spencer
Printed in the United States of America

dressystem.com

DRES system

holobi.

To all those who want to take their image
beyond trends and build a personal brand

CONTENTS

INTRODUCTION

By Margaret Spencer

"Growing into your future...requires a dedication to caring for yourself as if you were rare and precious, which you are, and regarding all life around you as equally so, which it is."

—Victoria Moran

In the summer of 2007, we had just relocated to the Seattle area for my husband's job. My daughters were eight and twelve, and starting to become aware of their bodies. I remember how concerned I was that they were being critical of their bodies and how I felt about my shape at that age. I saw how fashion magazines were starting to label women as "pears" and "apples" and did not feel this was a good model to teach to my young daughters. So I decided to create a body-typing system that would allow girls and women to feel more pride in their unique body shape and be comfortable in their own skin.

Wanting women to value their diverse body shapes, I decided to base the shapes on precious gems and came up with the **D**iamond **R**uby **E**merald **S**apphire, also known as "DRES System." I had no idea back then how this would take off and how quickly women would adopt their gem shape into their body identity and vocabulary.

You are born with a specific skeletal body shape that does not change. Even with weight gain or loss, most people will remain the same DRES body shape. In fact, you will most likely gain weight in the same place as others with your body shape. An easy way to figure out your shape is to look at where your body puts on weight first.

Gains weight evenly and maintains a small waist = **Diamond**

Gains weight in chest, arms, and bust = **Ruby**

Gains weight evenly or more around the waist = **Emerald**

Gains weight in hips and thighs = **Sapphire**

A more precise way to learn about your body shape is through a personal stylist. We use the DRES System to not only assess your shape, but identify your unique proportions using a math-based process. We identify a woman's gem-shaped figure primarily to build body acceptance and then teach women the most flattering styles for their shape. The goal is to embrace your shape and look for styles that not only flatter but fit well. Once you figure out what these styles are, you can start to build a wardrobe that will make you feel confident in anything you wear.

Using my background as a Graphic Designer and Art Director, I developed a style guide that would take the mystery out of determining your shape. This style guide uses math formulas and illustrates what styles to look for based on your body type. We initially thought this style guide, by itself, would solve women's problems of not knowing what to wear. Instead, through my market research, we learned that half of the women wanted someone to help them with their wardrobe and the other half wanted to learn how they could become a personal wardrobe stylist.

With this feedback, I built a process of styling that would not only make it simpler for the client to understand, it even makes learning how to become a Personal Stylist easier as well. Next, I developed our DRES Tools and professional Personal Color Analysis System that we use in private personal styling appointments—offering the best solutions that take the stress out of wardrobe management. In 2008, I opened the DRES Stylist Academy so I could share this system with other women wanting to open their own style consulting business.

After teaching this system, it became clear that it was not always easy to find the fit our clients were seeking. So in March of 2012, I ran a crowdfunding campaign on Kickstarter and raised funds to manufacture dresses based on the DRES System that highlight women's diverse body shapes. During this campaign, a slogan emerged: A Bigger Mission.

The Bigger Mission was about how clothes make us feel about ourselves; it was not really about the clothing itself. This campaign was an experiment to see how women would respond to clothing built for their shape. The results were increased self-acceptance and joy in finally finding clothes that fit.

When we try on clothes that do not fit us correctly, we assume our bodies are flawed in some way. We feel less-than, or not enough. This, combined with the digitally enhanced images that barrage us every day, leads us to feel that we are inadequate.

My message with the DRES clothing line is:

It's not that you don't fit the clothes;
it's that the clothes don't fit you!

We are all unique and this uniqueness has great value that should be celebrated. We should never let anything dull our shine. Having clothes that fit us properly brings out our confidence.

Being a DRES Personal Stylist is really about helping people reach their full potential. We see beauty in people and love to show them their beauty. When we help people to see the best in themselves, we enhance how they are perceived by others. This has a deep effect on the way they feel about themselves.

One of my greatest joys in life is inspiring others. Through this DRES business, I have had the opportunity to do more of this than ever before. It's really about women helping women and taking that confidence and paying it forward. The greatest compliment anyone can give me is not on my outfit, but that I have inspired them. This brings me great pride and joy.

Our DRES Stylists are on A Bigger Mission as well. Each of them represents DRES with a shared vision that goes beyond the basics of personal styling taught in our DRES System Certification course. Lisa Fischer is our Director of Education as well as a sought-out speaker on style and body image who spreads this message of self-value with poise and skill. Lori Goddard-Weed is our Director of Events and an integral part of the DRES organization, putting on workshops and special events to share our mission. Giselle Royston is a strong leader who has styled for celebrities. Mary Angelosante brings style and grace to everything she does. Wendy Petersen is a very talented and ambitious Stylist. I am so grateful for these ladies. The DRES organization attracts Personal Stylists with big hearts and a shared vision. We are so proud to have such an amazing group of women as co-authors of this book.

For our clients, A Bigger Mission means that they feel cared for and valued. They know that they can count on DRES Stylists to help them with their fashion needs, as well as their body image. Feeling fantastic about yourself is a natural result of the care and attention to detail that we provide.

Two years ago, I co-authored a book with some of our DRES Stylists called,

The Power of DRES. We shared tips and techniques of personal style. This time, I wanted us to write a book that goes beyond fashion tips. I wanted a real plan—real tools for confidence. This book is the answer. In it, six personal stylists share solutions so you can look and feel your best. You will gather insights on building confidence so you can be the best version of you.

It is my hope that this book transcends the practical advice of dressing and speaks to the benefits of inspiration, communication and confidence that styling can bring. If a picture is worth a thousand words, then a first impression is worth a billion. It communicates how you feel about yourself. Getting dressed should be a fun tool for self-expression, allowing your creative side to take over and try new things. It is only when you have gone beyond the superficial benefits of dressing that you can enjoy the intangible benefits of styling.

"It's also helpful to realize that this very body that we have, that's sitting right here, right now...with its aches and its pleasures...is exactly what we need to be fully human, fully awake, fully alive."

—Pema Chodron

CHAPTER 1

PERSONAL PERCEPTIONS

By Margaret Spencer

Have you ever felt misunderstood, misjudged, or labeled? You have one view of yourself, and others have a completely different view. I find it interesting how some of the smallest things we say and do influence others' perceptions of us—and at the same time how these small things are perceived differently by different people.

Simply telling someone what you do for a living can conjure up all kinds of associations they attach to you. Looking at your appearance may make them think things like, "You don't look old enough to be a doctor," or, "You're a minister?" or, "I would have never guessed."

Take for instance personal stylists. When we meet people and tell them what we do, the typical response is often an immediate excuse relating to their image. It ranges from "I just got back from working out…" to "I usually don't look this way."

What most people do not understand is we are not here to judge you. We're in this business to help people be their best selves. We study the expression on your face. What we do notice is when you are shining from within because the most important thing you can wear is your confidence.

As DRES Personal Stylists, we show people their beauty. We help them recognize their strongest features and bring them out. We help them shift the way they perceive their bodies. Most importantly, we help them feel confident in their figures through smart, strategic wardrobe choices that enable them to build pride in their appearance.

When people look in the mirror, it lies to them. What they typically see are an unrealistic amount of bumps, bulges, wrinkles, or other imperfections that are hardly visible to others. Our eyes zoom to those areas, checking to see if our imperfections still exist. We have been conditioned to hold ourselves to the unrealistic high standards of the beauty industry and media, resulting in feeling we are not good enough and do not measure up. Each glance in the mirror chips away at our confidence.

The truth, that most people do not realize, is no one else sees you the way you see yourself. We are way too critical of ourselves. Other people see you as a whole. They see your best features, the best parts of your personality, and the energy you bring.

"What's important in a dress
is the woman who is wearing it."

—Yves Saint Laurent

Here's the secret to dressing your best: how you feel about yourself trumps what you wear. When working with a personal styling client, I often have the opportunity to explain that an item is not best for them due to color, shape, or style. Sometimes the client will enthusiastically respond, "But, I love it and feel so great when I wear it!" Then I say, "Keep it and wear it confidently."

If you feel beautiful in a garment, then how you feel overrides all other assessments we go through to determine if an article of clothing fits into your wardrobe. Just be sure to rock it!

How you feel about yourself shows up in your posture and energy. How you carry your body sends out messages of how you feel about yourself. If your shoulders are hunched over, you could be feeling down. If your shoulders are high, you may be feeling stressed. The energy you put out when you are around people can say you're full of excitement or it can say you are depressed. Try to be aware of the posture and energy you are wearing.

"It's not your job to like me, it's mine."

—Byron Katie

A few months ago, I read an article in *Self Magazine 2015* by Tatiana Boncompagni about a woman who realizes she is in need of a makeover. It is a story that reminded me of the power of perception and resonated with me as it is something we hear often from our clients.

"I should have been happy, but I wasn't. Worse, I didn't know why or what I could have done about it. I kept myself busy with the kids and the house so I didn't have to think about it. And so, I felt fine, but not good enough. Then I saw a photo my husband took of me and gasped. The woman in the photo looked old, middle class, and tired. Was that what I really looked like? And if so, why hadn't I noticed before?"

I'm sure we can all relate to seeing a photo of ourselves that shocked us. It brings up thoughts like, "Do I really look like this to other people and how can I improve my image?" Patricia Wexler, M.D., a dermatologist in New York City, helps us put this into a healthy perspective.

"We all have tricks when we look in the mirror," says Wexler. "You tilt your head one way, you focus on one thing and not something else. It's a protective mechanism. But when you look at a picture, it's very objective."

After the woman received a head-to-toe makeover, she made an important discovery. Here is what she said about her transformation:

"While beauty makeovers can't fix life's bigger problems, they can act as powerful catalysts. I was feeling better about myself, which helped me overcome fears that were holding me back in some way or another. You could say it took me finding my look to find my voice."

"Everybody has a part of her body that she doesn't like, but I've stopped complaining about mine because I don't want to critique nature's handiwork. My job is simply to allow the light to shine out of the masterpiece."

—Alfre Woodard

BUILD YOUR PERSONAL BRAND

Be uncommon and stand out.

A brand is something distinguished by a unique characteristic. Is there something distinguishing about you? What are your characteristics?

You can build your personal brand and find your true identity. When working with one of our DRES Personal Stylists, they help you build your signature style through a series of questions and assessments. Building a list of descriptors around what makes you unique brings clarity and helps you understand what makes you uncommon so you can develop your signature style.

How people experience and perceive your brand impacts how you feel about yourself, so be conscious about how you show up in the world. If you are not sure how people perceive you, then ask. We often assume our closest friends and family see us the way we see ourselves. Some people would be surprised at how they would be described by their loved ones.

To learn more about yourself, ask three people close to you these questions:

1) How do you describe me to other people?

2) What is something you like about my appearance?

3) What is unique about me?

My friend Lisa Hufford wrote a small, yet impactful, book called *Be You: Five Steps to Living Your Personal Brand*. In it she writes, "Your personal brand is how your family, friends, and co-workers experience you. Your personal brand is reflected by how you communicate, dress, and live your life. Your personal brand is your strength plus your passion. Confidence is about remembering what you have done well in the past and owning it in your future."

Here are three excellent points she makes in her book:

- "Unique" means knowing how you stand out, your strengths and what is effortless for you.
- Be aware of how you communicate nonverbally.
- Your brand is your passions and interests.

"Self confidence is the best outfit,
rock it and own it."

—Unknown

CONFIDENCE

One of the things we pride ourselves on at DRES is helping others to feel more confidence through building their image and personal brand. It doesn't end there, though. We also help people to see their inner beauty and value. You may be wondering how we do this. First, let's take a look at what things build confidence:

- Positive feedback from others
- A series of successes
- Having a good relationship with yourself
- Bringing joy to others
- Adjusting your mindset

Positive Feedback

When you get a compliment it gives you a sense that you did something well and you feel happy. Positive feedback from others makes us feel good about ourselves, which in turn makes us feel more confident. This is why I encourage people to give compliments out freely. We often think that we like something about someone when we see them but don't verbalize it. Next time you notice something you like, let someone know. You might make their day.

Successes

From past experience I can tell you that having a series of successes can really bring up your confidence level. When I was starting out as a Graphic Designer in my field, I was unsure I could create designs that people would like. At first I realized I needed to prove myself, not only to the people I was working for, but to myself as well. Once I had a few successful projects under my belt, my confidence soared. Not only did my skill level strengthen, I also saw the difference in the way people treated me. I learned that you have to believe in yourself first before others can believe in you.

Relationship with Yourself

Often people give a lot of effort to nurture the relationships in their lives and neglect the relationship they have with themselves. You may wonder, how can you have a relationship with yourself? This is how you treat yourself and how you talk to yourself silently. Work on treating yourself with the same respect you want from others and you will see how this transforms the way you are treated. You have to love yourself before others can love you.

Bringing Joy

When you are not feeling very confident, try to find ways to bring joy to other peoples' lives. This is a surefire way to boost your confidence level. Giving to others makes us feel empowered and in turn, more confident. Spread the love and it will come back to you.

Confidence is really all about liking who you are and feeling self-assured. Some people are just naturally confident and others need to work at this. I believe it is possible to become the person you wish to be if you are willing to do the work it takes to get there.

You know, they say you should look carefully at the three people closest to you because you become like the people you hang around. This is greatly due to the influence they have over you. As humans we can be swayed by our friends and family as well as the media. We should take some time to consider and evaluate how we're being affected.

Adjusting Your Mindset

Every day we are influenced by outside forces and by what goes on in our minds. Self-talk can have more influence on how you act and what you attract than any other factor.

After doing extensive research on the topic of confidence over the years, I have developed a process for building it up through improving your mindset. It sets the stage for self-influence and taking control of your life. I offer you a simple process:

STEP 1: Complain

Start out by making a bulleted list of all of the things you do not like, or are unsatisfied about, in your life. This is your chance to be as negative as you want and really complain. When has anyone ever asked you to start complaining? Let it all out.

STEP 2: Simplify

Review your list and look for any items that can be consolidated or combined. Reduce this list down to the top ten things making you unhappy and that you want to change.

STEP 3: Translate

On a separate sheet of paper, write down the list of ten things that are negatives in your life. Now make a line to the right of that and on this side translate each negative into a positive. The new list should be positive things you want in your life.

STEP 4: Post

This list of positives has the power to become the biggest influence in your life if you use it right. Type this up, print it out on nice paper, and post it somewhere you will see it every day.

STEP 5: Practice

To build the muscles in your body you need to work them on a regular basis. Building your confident mindset is just the same: a positive mindset requires daily attention. Read this list to yourself daily for two months and then start to witness the transformation in yourself and your life.

Tip: To get the most out of this exercise, close your eyes and visualize how this will feel as if it has already occurred.

"Love yourself first and everything else falls into line. You really have to love yourself to get anything done in this world."

—Lucille Ball

BODY LANGUAGE

Your body language affects how others see you just as much as what you wear, and it doesn't cost you a cent. When thinking about our image we think about all the things we can put on our bodies. However, we rarely contemplate the nonverbal communication that stems from our posture and how we pose.

In her TED Talk, social psychologist Amy Cuddy says, "Your body language shapes who you are, body language affects how others see us, but it may also change how we see ourselves. 'Power posing'—standing in a posture of confidence, even when we don't feel confident—can affect testosterone and cortisol levels in the brain and might even have an impact on our chances for success."

Amy goes on to say, "We know our nonverbals govern how other people think and feel about us. But do our nonverbals govern how we think about ourselves? There is some evidence that says we do. When we are forced to smile by holding a pen in our teeth, we feel happier. When it comes to power, we feel more powerful when we put our hands on our hips and stand with our feet set wide apart. A power pose."

To prove this effect, Amy ran an experiment on a group of people using high-power poses. When they were in the high-power poses for two minutes, they experienced higher tendencies for risk tolerance, testosterone was increased by 20 percent and cortisol decreased by 20 percent. As a result, they were more assertive, confident and comfortable.

Next time you are going to speak in front of people or are being interviewed, try to do a few power poses two minutes right before you start.

"Don't fake it 'til you make it; fake it 'til you become it."

—Amy Cuddy

THE DRES SYSTEM

I created the DRES System of identifying body shapes as precious gems to instill value, self-worth, and pride in the uniqueness of each figure. The days of being labeled a "pear" or a "rectangle" are over! Our DRES Stylists are dedicated to improving the way women see their bodies; providing the highest quality services and tools to help them look and feel beautiful and confident.

The DRES System is a scientific, systematic approach to personal styling that empowers people to look and feel brilliant. It's based on four basic body shapes: Diamond, Ruby, Emerald, and Sapphire. Our core belief is that every woman is a precious gem and no matter what your body shape, size, or age, there is beauty within you just waiting to be revealed. Our DRES System training and Certified Personal Stylists help you connect to your brilliance by helping you create your personal DRES Profile to bring your outer image into alignment with your inner beauty.

The reason this system works is because of its simplicity and our unique personalization technique. Our goal is to provide you with the tools and support you need to curate a wardrobe that reflects your lifestyle. We want you to stand out as the unique individual you are.

Gem BODY Shapes

The gem body shapes were originally just developed for women, however we have extended this method to include men as well. Below you will find the descriptions for the female body shapes. When looking for your shape, remember you are looking for the one that you are most dominant in. Many people may be a combination of two, however there is always one that stands out most. Also, keep in mind there is more needed to assess your perfect fit than just body shape. When you meet with a personal stylist they will provide you with a full assessment and this will include exact shape assessment as well as proportion analysis.

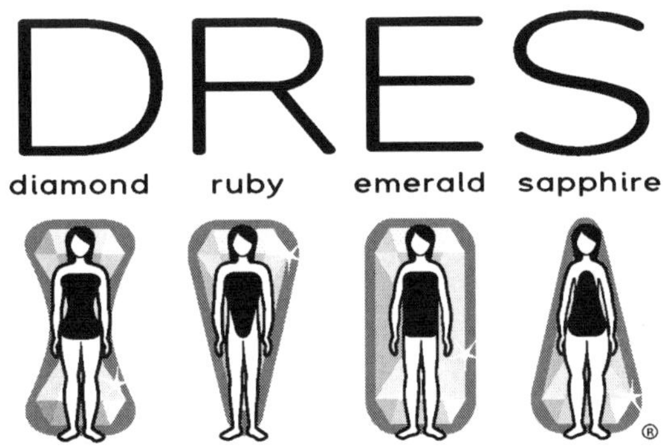

Diamond

The beauty of the Diamond body shape is in the symmetry and defined waistline. While you are starting out with a beautifully balanced body, you could lose this symmetry quickly with the wrong clothing and accessory choices. Look to widen the shoulders a little and show off your waist.

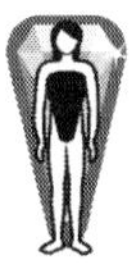

Ruby

The beauty of the Ruby body shape is in the slender hips and thighs. You either have a large bust line or broad shoulders. Create symmetry and balance in your shape with the right clothing and accessory choices. Look to reduce the chest and/or shoulder area and show off your legs.

Emerald

The beauty of the Emerald body shape is in the symmetry of the shoulders and hips. Your arms and legs are proportionate to the rest of your body. You could lose this symmetry quickly with the wrong clothing and accessory choices. Look to slim the waist and reveal your assets.

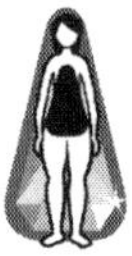

Sapphire

The beauty of the Sapphire body shape is in the slender arms and small rib cage. Your décolleté begs to be highlighted. Create symmetry and balance in your shape with appropriate clothing and accessory choices. Look to reduce the width of the hips and thigh area and show off your waist and arms.

DRES
system
"The compliments keep coming"
- Lori Goddard-Weed
Shape: Diamond
Style: Dramatic
Color: #7
Before

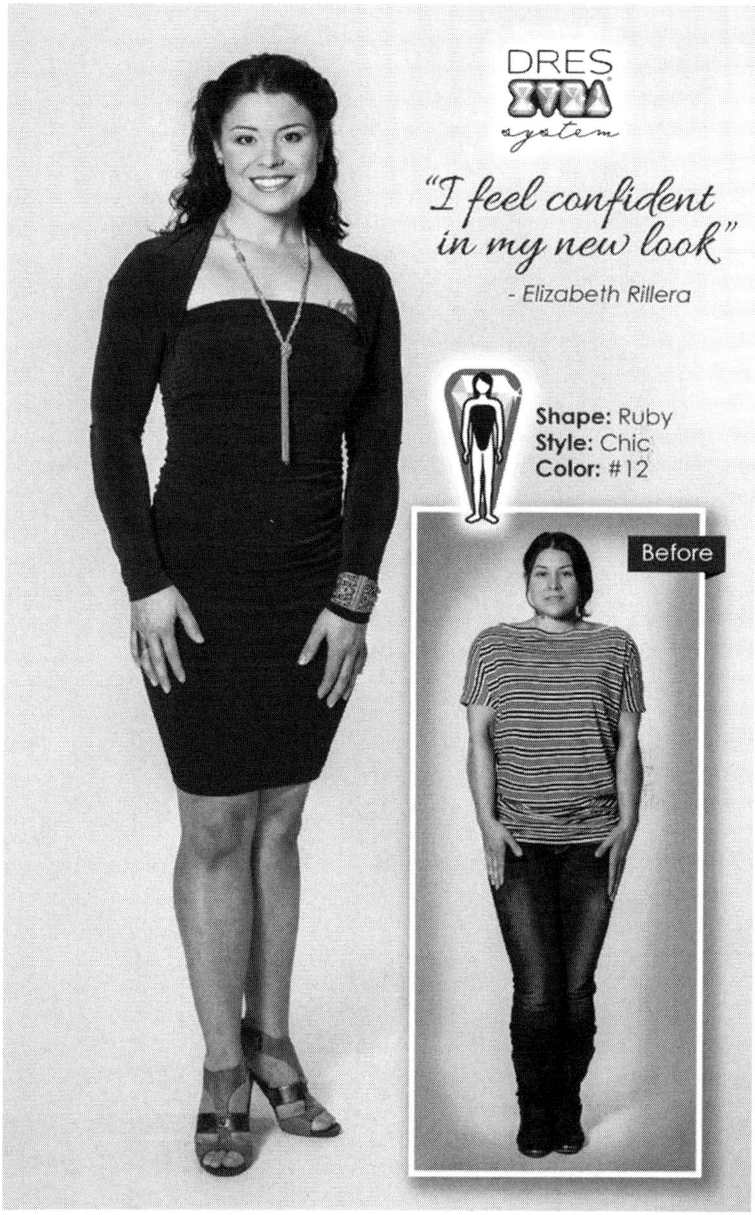
DRES
system
"I feel confident in my new look"
- Elizabeth Rillera
Shape: Ruby
Style: Chic
Color: #12
Before

"I got the job on the spot!"
- Lisa Fischer
Shape: Emerald
Style: Classic
Color: #11
Before

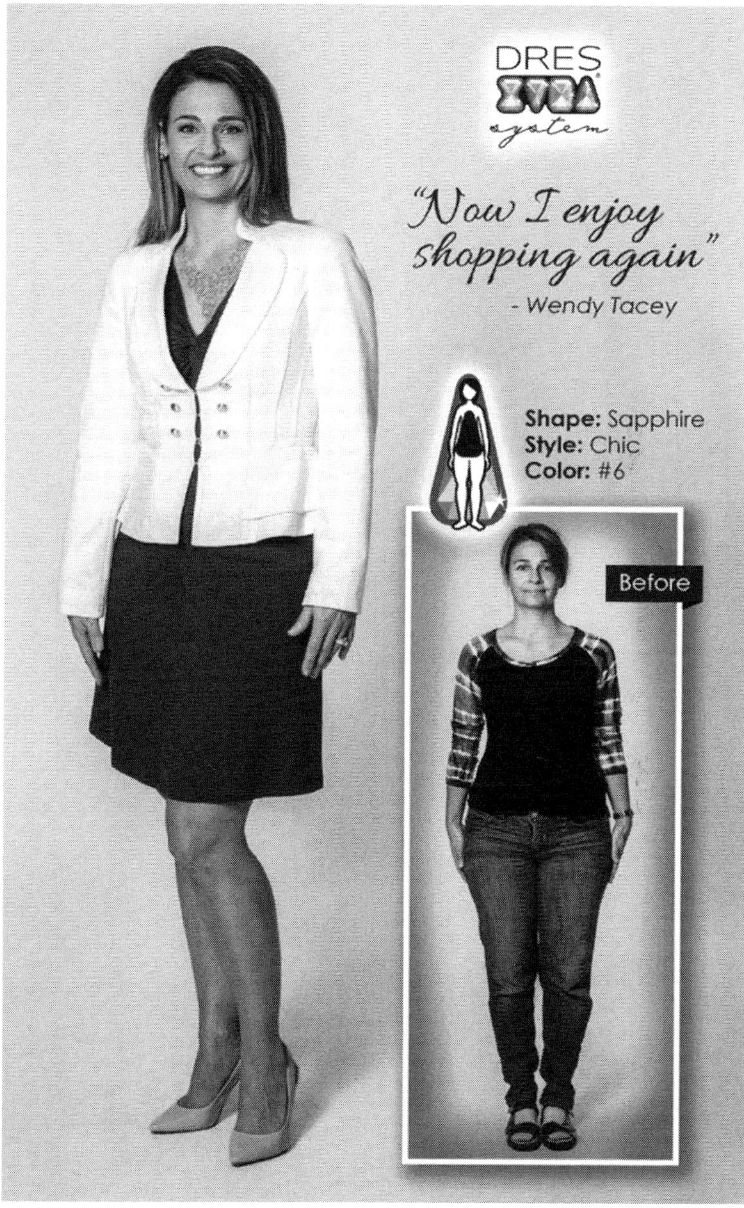
DRES
system
"Now I enjoy shopping again"
- Wendy Tacey
Shape: Sapphire
Style: Chic
Color: #6
Before

Gem Face Shapes

People are often confused by which face shape they have. To make this easy we have developed a math-based formula for determining your face shape. This identifies whether your face shape is a Diamond, Ruby, Emerald, or Sapphire and if it is long, short, or in the middle.

Diamond
Similar forehead and cheekbones with a narrower jawline

Ruby
Wider forehead than cheekbones with a narrower jawline

Emerald
Similar forehead, cheekbones, and jawline width

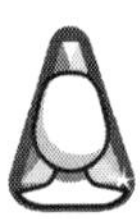

Sapphire
Narrower forehead than cheekbones with a wider jawline

Shape: Diamond
Style: Chic
Color: #9
DRES
system
Before

Shape: Ruby
Style: Classic
Color: #2
DRES
system
Before

Shape: Emerald
Style: Dramatic
Color: #11
Before
DRES
system

Shape: Sapphire
Style: Romantic
Color: #7
Before
DRES
system

"Girls of all kinds can be beautiful —from the thin, plus-sized, short, very tall, ebony to porcelain skinned, the quirky, clumsy, shy, outgoing and all in between. It's not easy though because many people still put beauty into a confining, narrow box...Think outside of the box...Pledge that you will look in the mirror and find the unique beauty in you."

—Tyra Banks

Fashion Styles

The five fashion styles help you create a refined image that reflects what you intend to project.

Your fashion style should first be authentic by aligning with your personality type. Second, it should be appropriate for the activity in which you are participating. Classic, Chic, Romantic, Ethnic, and Dramatic are the five fashion styles we use in the DRES System. Everyone has one fashion style that is most dominant. Can you easily identify yours?

Classic: gracious, refined, and sophisticated

Chic: modern, self-assured, and sharp

Romantic: friendly, casual, and whimsical

Ethnic: diverse, authentic, and cultural

Dramatic: energetic, exciting, and strong

DRES Color Palette

Professional color analysis is one of the most valuable services you can receive. It will help you select clothing that complements you. Simply wearing the right colors can make a huge difference in how you look and feel, and save you time shopping. Your Personal Stylist can define your 42 ultimate colors out of over 500 possibilities. We use our exclusive DRES System to provide a detailed analysis of your individual coloring, and create a personalized Color Palette with beautiful fabric swatches handmade just for you.

WHAT'S YOUR DRES CODE?

The DRES Code is simply your Personal DRES Profile turned into an acronym. It is a code that tells you if an item will work for you, narrows down the options, and expedites the selection process. The code has three elements:

1) Body Shape
2) Fashion Style
3) Color ID

This is an easy way to know if an item is going to work for your personal style before you even try it on, taking some of the guesswork out of shopping.

For example, if this is your profile:

Body Shape: **Ruby**

+

Fashion Style: **Chic**

+

Color ID: **8**

=

Your DRES Code would be: **RC8**

Not everyone fits nicely into just one area. Many people are a combination of these, however to make it easy on you we will want to find your dominant body shape, fashion style, and color range for your code. To unlock your DRES code, contact one of our DRES System Certified Personal Stylists. After a profile appointment you will walk away with a comprehensive assessment and personalized Style Guide.

Perhaps you have several items in your wardrobe that still have the tags on them from last season. This is a sign that you need clarity. Once you know more you can do better. Understanding and defining your unique proportions, coloring, and style will give you divine clarity. This will allow you to make wiser purchasing decisions because knowledge is power.

"Even the models we see in magazines
wish they could look like their own images."

—Cheri K. Erdman

BEYOND DRES

In the following chapters, you will find insights on being your best self and inspiration to improve your confidence. Each chapter is written by one of our DRES System Certified Personal Stylists. This is a collection of perspectives on why they see a bigger mission for personal styling than just dressing people fashionably. These ladies have heart, passion, and commitment to help you look and feel your best. Sit back and enjoy as our top Personal Stylists open up about the secrets and lessons learned in the fashion business.

"I'm a bookkeeper so I'm not great with **anything** *artistic, including dressing myself. Margaret was able to come into my home and, in three visits, I had a different view and a more positive outlook. It even inspired me to go on a diet, and I've lost 30 pounds so far! The experience was a little scary. But I was made comfortable by Margaret's calm, reassuring manner and relaxed approach to the DRES System. I now go into my closet and am better able to pick out what to wear without it causing me anxiety or stress."*

— Linda Cavanaugh (Sapphire)

Margaret Spencer
Founder and Creator of DRES System

Seattle, Washington
ms@dressystem.com
dressystem.com

Margaret has always been drawn to excellent design and appreciates high-quality materials. With a degree in Visual Communications, she has had a career as a Graphic Designer, Illustrator, and Creative Director. In her free time, she enjoys painting oversized abstract paintings, interior decorating, and the great outdoors.

She is fascinated with the beauty found in the world around her and the people within it. With a lifelong pursuit of entrepreneurial ventures, in 2007 she chose to build a business that would make a positive difference in the world by using fashion to elevate women's self-confidence.

Her entrepreneurial journey has resulted in training and certifying over seventy-five women on the DRES System; traveling all over the US to speak and teach; publishing her first co-authored book, *The Power Of DRES*; and running a successfully crowdfunded Kickstarter campaign (kickstarter.com), raising almost $22K in thirty days to manufacture dresses based on the DRES System Program.

Now Margaret focuses her creative energy, passion for design, and entrepreneurial drive on growing and sharing the power of the DRES System. Drawing from all her past experiences, she gives women the best tools and support to instill self-worth and acceptance of their bodies. She knows first-hand how women can struggle with how to dress their figures and feel confident in their individual images.

"I wish for you what I wish for myself—
the opportunities to reach your fullest potential."

—Margaret Spencer

CHAPTER 2

IMAGE ALIGNMENT

By Lisa Fischer

"I used to think confidence came from what other people thought about me—but now I realize (it) comes from what I feel about myself."

—Demi Lovato

One of the many lessons I've learned working as a wardrobe stylist is to recognize the power of nonverbal communication. The way in which you clothe your body, groom yourself, and how you accessorize gives the world a clue to who you are, what you value, and even how you want to be treated. It's your billboard that speaks before you do. The great revelation is you don't have to love shopping, jewelry, or any part of getting dressed. The secret weapon is knowing that clothing is one of many tools to create an intentional, powerful, and authentic visual message.

This is true of my own personal journey. My young years were times of poverty, adversity, and upheaval. My sense of style was nonexistent as a teen. As a young careerist, I looked to co-workers and copied fashions for the industry. Baseball hats and sweats became my go-to style during child-raising years. My style transformation evolved in my mid-forties out of the need to show up in truth and authenticity.

I've worked diligently to discover my own style: one that reflects who I am, unencumbered by anyone else's opinion or voice. Today, I walk into any venue in any arena of my life and feel confident, authentic, and appropriate.

From the many lessons and experiences learned, I am passionately committed to helping women feel triumphant in their appearance and style. Achieving visual mastery is a process. The following pages will provide a framework to help you get started on your own image and confidence journey. My hope is you will enjoy the tips, stories, and exercises within this chapter and feel empowered to take action.

Framework topics we will review are:

- Discover your identifiable personal brand
- Know your wardrobe style
- Create a style statement
- Choose wardrobe pieces to flatter your unique shape
- Discover the colors that enhance your eyes, hair, and skin tone
- Add accessories to build a signature look

As a Wardrobe Stylist and the Director of Education for the DRES System, I often get questions about the subject of personal and professional branding. Companies, groups, and individuals want to ensure they are representing their best selves always. The majority of questions seem centered around how to achieve a congruent and consistent brand.

I believe confidence is strengthened by living life with authenticity—who you are, what you value, and your own unique purpose.

The intent of the next section is to provoke "food for thought" on the process of developing your brand. You may find using a journal helpful as you develop your roadmap for discovery.

So here we go...let's get started.

POWER OF PERSONAL BRAND

A personal brand is in many ways synonymous with your reputation. It refers to the way other people see you and perceive your character, purpose, passion, and attitude. When you have a personal brand, people recognize and care about your name, what you're working on, what you offer, and what you're about.

You are your brand. Your brand is your personality, how you communicate, the contribution you make in the world, and your actions. All these elements influence the first impression others have of you and the intuition they experience in your presence. We all know first impressions are made within the first few seconds of meeting someone. It's human nature to evaluate someone on our own scale of professionalism, attractiveness, relatability, credibility, trustworthiness, attention to detail, and likeability.

My friend Sundi has one of the most identifiable brands I've experienced in business. She is a successful business woman. She is physically beautiful and is extremely personable. Sundi is fit, eats healthy, has a positive mindset, works hard, and truly cares about other people's success. If you were to analyze her physical attractiveness, most women may feel jealous of her strong and curvy physique. Yet, her body is not the number-one criteria of her personal brand. Her brand is modest, polished, and serving focused—always! In business, her look is pulled together, sharp, modest, and poised, complete with statement jewelry pieces.

I'm drawn to Sundi's outgoing and caring personality. I appreciate how Sundi shows up consistently in her visual presentation and values. Colleagues constantly comment on what an amazing person she is and how much they enjoy her. Sundi is a great example of personal and professional brand mastery.

BUILDING A RECOGNIZABLE PERSONAL BRAND

In preparation to building a framework for your own personal brand, I'm going to ask you to answer the following questions. My hope is your answers will bring awareness and clarity as you build upon your brand design.

Recall a time you walked into a room and someone in the group really stood out to you. Can you recall the feelings you had when you saw that person? What do you admire about that individual?

When you walk into a room, what are the messages (perceptions) you want others to associate with you?

Equally as important, what are messages (perceptions) that you* don't *want associated with you?

Where do you want to be professionally in five years?

What are you passionate about?

What are your strengths?

What do you value?

What areas in your life do you want to improve?

Your answers to the above questions add to the framework of your personal brand. Review them often.

KNOWING YOUR PERSONALITY

Another component to creating an authentic visual image/brand is to be mindful of your personality traits and characteristics.

If you've ever taken a personality test, such as the Myers-Briggs Type Indicator personality inventory, you know the importance of your identified strengths and gifts.

I recall several years ago when I was teaching an afterschool program for elementary-age children. I thought the best wardrobe would be something that communicated high authority since I wanted the children's attention. Boy was I wrong. For months, early on in my teaching career, I struggled to connect with the kids. My need for fun, connection, and influence were not being met. I was frustrated and felt I must not have what it takes to be an effective teacher. After an exhaustive period of trial and error, I began to unveil the disconnect. I was shocked to realize how my nonverbal messaging was the obstacle keeping me from my ability to effectively connect.

The visual image I was portraying with my black suit, white collar, pearls, and pumps was ultra conservative and highly professional. My vibrant personality was being overshadowed by my appearance. I appeared authoritative and dominant versus approachable and influential. My fun, friendly, outgoing personality was stuck behind a black suit. The better wardrobe for my desired outcome included softer colors, along with comfortable trousers and blouses. Note to self: know your audience.

A Look Inside

So, how about you? Let's take some time to discuss your personality. Here's a list of words to get you started. (This is not an exhaustive list...expand and do some homework here.) Circle the words that resonate as you reflect on your personality:

conservative	charismatic
bold	humble
sophisticated	compassionate
charming	vibrant
fun	optimistic
timeless	critical
direct	empathetic
modern	inquisitive
gentle	artistic
adventurous	sincere
intense	sharp-witted
elegant	predictable
edgy	spontaneous
sensitive	reserved
kind	approachable
artistic	formal
dynamic	informal
independent	extrovert
free-spirited	introvert
adaptable	intuitive

Ask for Feedback

If you're finding you'd like additional input, it can be interesting to get positive feedback from others whose opinion you value. *Caution: This is an exercise to be shared with people you trust and whose raw opinion you value.* You can simply photocopy the above word list and circle the words they'd use to describe your personality. Personally, I have found this to be an invaluable exercise.

YOUR OWN UNIQUENESS

Let's Consider Personal Style

Have you ever gone clothes shopping and come across an item that reminded you of someone? What was it about the item that made the association for you? Was it the style, design, or perhaps the color of an item? Associations around these design elements are powerful and can become part of your brand.

Style is a form of self-expression using wardrobe, grooming, and accessories.

Two common statements I hear my clients say during a consultation are, "I have no style" or "I like so many things, I don't know where to begin." This is usually followed by feeling overwhelmed and confused.

Just like a flower has personality and evokes a variety of feelings, so does fashion. Let's visualize two pairs of sunglasses. One offers a plain gold wire rim with rounded, amber lenses. The other includes a jeweled, embellished frame with squared, black lenses. Each style will resonate with a certain type of person, often linked to lifestyle and personality.

Over the years, designers have set themselves apart for their brand and style, which fall within a mix of industry terminology for fashion styles. Margaret covers this beautifully in her chapter. In review, they are Classic, Chic, Romantic, Ethnic and Dramatic.

To expand on what Margaret has covered regarding fashion styles, take a look at the conveyed messages of each style. Do you see familiar words that you associate with your brand? This will help steer you towards your personal style in your image journey.

Fashion Style	Wardrobe Description	Conveyed Messages
Classic	Tailored lines, structured shapes, timeless quality	Refined, poised, sophisticated, formal
Chic	Modern flair, edgy, contemporary style	Outgoing, striking, credible, bold
Romantic	Soft, flowing shapes, feminine detailing	Gracious, charming, caring, sensitive
Ethnic	Comfortable, natural fabrics, practical	Carefree, cultural, relaxed, playful, cultivating
Dramatic	Bold, geometric shapes, statement pieces	Powerful, dynamic, intense, modern, direct

Create Your DRES System Style Statement

My experience teaching elementary-age students was my wakeup call to the fact I was walking through life presenting an image completely opposite of who I was and the characteristics I want to be known for. Why did everything I purchase look sterile and boring? I bought "appropriate" clothes without regard to my messaging. I thought I had to sacrifice personal style for a plain, corporate look.

A style statement is an affirmation and a written blueprint stating your desired image outcome. This outcome can be one you already possess or are in the process of creating.

Style statement exercise: Take a minute to intentionally create a statement of style. The Look Inside exercise and the words from your Personal Style Chart have given you a strong base with which to begin. In a moment, I'll invite you to choose your top three words and write them as an affirmation statement.

As you consider the words from your previous exercise, be aware of the emotions each word brings forth. Which words feel more authentic? Which words build into your vision of how you want to show up?

As an example, here's my style statement: I am elegant, passionate, and inspirational.

As I sit with the meaning of these words, I visualize myself feeling confident. When I am with others, I visualize a poised self with strong interest in those around me. I am thoughtful in my word choices. I consider appropriate wardrobe for the occasion and have positive language to uplift those around me. I share my visions, hopes, dreams, and desires with those whose life it enriches.

Your turn to share your style statement: I am...

Did you write your style statement down? Remember, you'll move closer to your goal when you write, speak, visualize, and feel the attainment of living your style statement.

Visualize your wardrobe, your hair, your accessories, your posture, your activities, and your lifestyle. How do others respond to you? What does it look like to live your personal style statement?

If you were in my bathroom you would see my style statement written in bold letters on my mirror. It's the first and last thing I see after getting ready in the morning. It's actually a fun exercise!

POWER OF BODY SHAPE

Have you ever gone shopping with a friend and felt that she has it so much easier than you? Does everything look better when she tries it on? General awesomeness around a successful shopping experience and creating a particular look comes from knowing your body shape, skin tone, fashion style, and clothing size.

The subject of shape can be a sensitive one. The word "shape" brings up memories that may have been locked away for years, as well as uncomfortable feelings of comparison, judgment, or even inadequacy. Recently I was invited to speak on the subject of personal style for a women's golf club. During the introduction, the president mentioned I would be assessing everyone's body shape. Every face went blank. Some guests looked down at the floor while others gasped and said, "Oh God." Some simply laughed out loud!

I realized then how "off limits" the subject of body shape can be for many individuals. I've watched women grab at their stomach, butt, hips, bust, and the fleshy part of their arms as if to say, "I'm dissatisfied."

My belief is every person is unique, special, and beautiful. I love discussing body shape and the diversity of each woman's curves. My job is to provide style techniques that create visual mastery for my clients. There is nothing more thrilling than to watch a woman realize the fullness of her physical beauty. The education process and "aha" moments my clients experience keep me doing what I love.

Becky's Story

Becky is a client I met while hosting a style workshop at a local boutique. She came to the event feeling anxious, self-conscious, and fearful of hating the experience. She made herself attend out of desperation. Her marriage was suffering, she had a major case of "frumpy" and, quite frankly, she was ready to give up. We went to work!

I pulled items for Becky's Ruby body shape, warm skin tone, and large size. The items de-emphasized Becky's wide shoulders and large bust while bringing interest to her lower body. One of the key components to style confidence is balancing and bringing symmetry to the silhouette. Putting together mix-and-match pieces were important to Becky. The "aha" moment I will always remember was Becky seeing herself in the mirror for the first time with her new style. I'll always remember her words, "Oh my God, I look beautiful!"

WARDROBE THAT FLATTERS

Here are a few things to know about a flattering look.

1) Fit Is Key

Clothes that are too tight or too baggy can make you appear bigger and will draw attention to that area of the body. Quite often during a client closet edit, I will find baggy and shapeless tops that were previously purchased to cover a wide hip, tummy, or bum area. The better choice is to choose garments that flatter and skim the curves, versus hiding and covering up your shape.

2) Mastery of Tailoring

Do you know that most clothing pieces are designed around a fit model's body and proportions? It is not unusual for a garment to need attention and tailoring since the majority of us are not professional models. If you find a wardrobe piece you love and it fits the "hard to fit" part of your body, but is too big in other areas, consider having the piece tailored. For example, one of my clients is broad shouldered and large busted. A fabulous jacket for her is one that first fits the bust line comfortably without gaping. Second, adding a small shoulder pad offsets her large bust line. Lastly, taking in the sides make the jacket fit her torso nicely. Simple tailor fixes include: hemline adjustment; eliminating gapping in the back part of the waistband, shoulder seam, baggy shirt, or jacket; and shortening sleeves that are too long.

3) Proportions Matter

Bringing the body shape into symmetry and balance is a key objective when dressing. I've never yet met with a woman who hired me to help her look heavier or shorter. The goal is to maximize your assets and bring balance to your shape. Let's say you have a short torso with long legs. A style trick to elongate the appearance of your torso is to wear longer, fitted tops and long jackets. Also, choose light-colored tops with vertical seaming or a pattern. To elongate a short leg, keep the garment darker in color, creased with the hemline no higher than one inch from the floor. A pointed toe is critical here to keep the elongation of the silhouette.

POWER OF COLOR

Color is said to have many functions including stirring and evoking emotion. We associate colors to many of our favorite brands. When we are in the mood for a cup of coffee and a place to sit with friends, we know the warm hues of a coffee shop draw us in. When the toddlers are hungry, we look for the red and gold sign of McDonalds along the state highway. While traveling, we can become overwhelmed by the beauty of a sunset over an ocean beach.

Color worn on the body evokes emotion and physical reaction. Color can make someone appear authoritative, regal, sexy, happy, approachable, and energetic—to name a few. Color can also be used to enhance or camouflage features on the body. Light colors draw our attention, where darker colors diminish attention.

The area of color I find the most interesting when working with a client is the difference between what looks fabulous "on" an individual and the colors they like to "see."

For example, prior to becoming a wardrobe stylist, I had my colors analyzed by Margaret Spencer. I thought this was going to be a breeze. I knew all the best colors on me. After all, people had been complimenting me on my clothes for years. I considered myself an expert on what looked good on me.

Oh what a huge learning opportunity! During our appointment, I recall Margaret selecting exotic deep colors such as burnt orange, copper, and green. Seriously? I remember questioning her qualifications and education around color. If you were to step into my closet back then, you would find simplicity. Everything was black and white. I had absolutely no pops of color other than possibly a few grey dresses and beige tops. Well, there was a chartreuse dress I loved, but it was edited out of the closet because the color overpowered me and made my skin look dull and washed out.

I'll never forget Margaret's words, "Lisa, black and white together do not serve you like these deep, rich, warm tones." She suggested that if I liked black and white so much that I may want to consider decorating a room in my house with those colors. That's exactly what I did.

If only you could see me at this moment. I'm sitting with my laptop at my black lacquer dining room table, the walls are white with red accents, and the floors are grey marble. I love it!

Margaret was right. I've learned it's one thing to look at colors and enjoy the feeling that comes from viewing them (I feel elegant and modern in my dining room). It's another thing to wear color and know how the color accentuates or detracts from your hair, eyes, and skin. When I wear black and white, the colors show up before I do. My skin is warm-toned. I have soft brown eyes with gold flecks, and my hair is light brown with golden highlights.

So, what about the compliments I would receive on my light-grey jacket or black-and-white tops? The awareness I have come to is this: are people complimenting my jacket or are they complimenting me? Think about a time when someone complimented you on how nice *you* looked. Think to another time when someone said how much they liked your shirt. There's a big difference.

YOUR ULTIMATE COMPLEMENTARY COLORS

Always and without fail, any time you wear your natural body tones closest to your face you will appear radiant and "pulled together." Be objective when considering the tones of your skin, blush, eye color (and the flecks within), along with your natural hair colors.

Harmonizing your wardrobe pieces with your personal coloring is the glue that pulls a look together.

I'll often hear ladies say they know their best coloring because they've already had their colors professionally analyzed and they are a "particular season." That terminology alone gives away the last time they probably had their colors reviewed, and it's not recent. When I question the last time they've had their colors evaluated, for most it's been several years and they just found their color fan in an old box when moving.

If you've had your colors analyzed before, congratulations! You are in the driver's seat for creating an amazing image. However, if it's been a decade ago or even longer, it's time to update. As we mature, our skin tone changes along with our hair color. The colors that once served us may not look as flattering as they used to. In fact, a lot of the colors may be highlighting the very facial imperfections we are trying to conceal with cosmetics.

I know when I wear pure white today I feel a need to wear heavier makeup because the brightness of the white washes me out and highlights my adult acne and sun damage spots. The interesting thing about white is it's brighter than the brightest color and stands out when paired with any other color. What does that mean for you?

If your teeth and/or the whites of your eyes are yellowing—pure white will only make those features appear more discolored than they are. It's like a big neon sign saying, "Look at my stained teeth." It's so true! I've decided to whiten my teeth professionally because I enjoy red wine and coffee and won't be giving them up any time soon.

Think back to your style statement while reading this section on color psychology. When you plan style, fit, and color, you are showing up intentionally and with purpose. Here are some thoughts to add purpose to your wardrobe with color:

Colors	Attributes and Messaging
Black	authoritative, official, formal
Brown	reliable, steady, receptive
White	graceful, elegant, innocent, formal
Charcoal	credible, stable, powerful, capable
Red	powerful, exciting, assertive
Pink	gentle, friendly, approachable
Blue	trustworthy, dependable, calm
Green	creative, generous, progressive
Yellow	cheerful, optimistic, fun
Orange	ambitious, creative, energetic
Purple	refined, sophisticated, elegant

Having this chart at your fingertips will help you in your brand development. The three components to an amazing outfit are fit, style, and color. Coordinating your wardrobe with your ultimate neutrals, darks, lights, metallic, and fashion colors is the key for a winning appearance.

Color assessment has come a long way since the era of the four seasons. Today's most effective color review is done by custom analysis of your hair, eye, and skin tone. My clients love their customized color palette and don't leave home without it!

Pollie's Story

Pollie is a client of mine in her mid-fifties. She is a wife, sister, grandmother, and flight attendant in Seattle. When she hired me to do a color analysis, her closet at the time reflected many bright and cool colors (purples, pinks, light blues). Pollie is a happy, cheerful person and these colors made her feel happy. However, she was frustrated by constantly feeling washed out and having to overcompensate with cosmetics to help her feel colorful. Pollie has warm skin, blonde hair with golden lowlights, and brown hazel eyes.

After she received her custom color palette of hand-selected colors based on her natural coloring, Pollie now feels relaxed when pulling together her outfits because she's confident about wearing the most flattering colors.

Recently while on vacation in Paris, she purchased some beautiful scarves and wardrobe pieces in gorgeous, rich warm tones that she would never have chosen before. She was grateful to know what colors were the most flattering because it's not easy to return the items to Paris if she changed her mind.

YOU MAY LOVE THE COLOR BUT DOES IT LOVE YOU?

So, let's talk about you, your coloring, and your features.

For a moment, we need a clean slate. This is just you and me talking together. Let's put aside the compliments from others and the colors you chose for decorating your home. You need to disassociate yourself from your favorite college or pro team colors and the cute tops you are drawn to at the department store. This may be your first time to really think about color harmony and your personal coloring.

First, find a mirror and stand by a kitchen or bedroom window where you can get some good natural daylight. Study your eyes. What color are they? Do you see any flecks of color? Do you have dark circles?

Now look at your skin. What is your skin tone? Is there any color in the blush area of your cheeks? Is there any discoloration or overall coloring of skin?

Now, notice the color of your hair. Do you see multiple colors or is there only one dominant shade?

What do you notice from this exercise? When I first went through this evaluation, I was amazed. I discovered my eyes have rich flecks of gold, copper, and brown. My skin is much warmer than I thought and my hair has lightened over the years.

Let's keep going. While in front of the mirror, hold up articles of clothing from your closet. A simple test is to close your eyes, bring the clothing to your face, and then open your eyes. What did you see first? Do you see the color of the clothing or your beautiful features? The goal is for you and your features to take center stage, not the colors of your clothing. This may take some practice, but it is a good tip for doing a home self-analysis.

I would recommend a professional color assessment from a trained and certified image consultant who specializes in color services. This is especially helpful if you struggle with color blindness or simply find this subject difficult. You can find more information at www.dressystem.com. With our styling service, you will receive a personalized fan of ultimate colors to help you shop and coordinate outfits with ease.

Wearing Your Ultimate Colors

Wearing colors that are harmonious with your personal coloring is key to a masterful look.

In general, if your eye color is brown, green, or hazel with gold color flecks and you have golden highlights in your hair, colors in the warm family are going to complement you well. This includes but is not limited to green, gold, yellow, orange, peach, rust red, copper, bronze, and brown.

If your eyes are blue with grey flecks and you have rosy cheeks and black, blonde, or grey hair—colors in the cool family are going to complement you well. This includes but is not limited to pink, purple, plum, wine, rose, apple red, blue, platinum, and silver.

SHOP YOUR CLOSET

Have you ever stood half naked in front of your closet and said these words, "I have nothing to wear." Have you said these words while looking at a closet stuffed full of clothing?

You are not alone. The majority of clients I work with wear approximately 20 percent of their wardrobe over and over again.

So...what's up with the other 80 percent?

I have personally found this to be a fascinating subject and I'm always curious to hear the answer from women I work with.

Here are some personal, real-life answers as to why the remaining 80 percent of wardrobe hangs untouched:

"I bought it on sale."

"Not sure and the price tag is still on it."

"I felt pressured by the sales associate."

"My husband (or mother) bought it for me, I can't possibly give it away."

"It looked really cute on the mannequin."

"I had a gift certificate and had to spend it."

"My friend wears this style."

"Too big" or "too small"

"What's in my closet is too big or too small, as a matter of fact I have three different sizes going on in my closet."

"I just liked it."

"I got it on a cruise."

"The color is pretty."

"It's perfect for my industry I work in, but it's not me. It makes me look ___________."

"It has sentimental value. I wore it in high school."

Need I go on?

If you related to any of those statements, do not worry. When Margaret was in my closet, I stated about half of this list, so I'm the first one to say, "Guilty!"

Truly, the majority of clients have hundreds, if not thousands, of dollars of wardrobe hanging in their closet, unused.

The price of hiring a wardrobe stylist to do a closet edit is around the price of a haircut and foil, which never compares to the dollars invested in a wardrobe that isn't being worn. Truly, it boils down to the magical components of fit, style, size, and coloring based upon your intentional messaging to the world. Getting these four areas to be your workhorse is essential. Then you can focus your energies on your life's priorities.

PSYCHOLOGY OF A WARDROBE EDIT

First, understand a wardrobe edit is personal. When I'm hired for a wardrobe edit, the first thing I will say is "no judgment." I'm the non-emotional girlfriend who is unbiased about your personal and professional history. I work through the lens of your personal style statement, fit, and ultimate coloring to build a foundation of pieces you love and can pull from daily—regardless of the occasion.

Take your valuable energy and focus on where you are going versus where you have been. If you need to keep some of the sentimental pieces that no longer serve you, that's fine. Just keep them in a bin and out of your closet.

ACCESSORY WISDOM

Most of us have heard that first impressions are made within the first several seconds of meeting someone. But have you heard the actual breakdown of the statistics? Studies say that 55 percent of a first impression is determined by the wearer's wardrobe, accessories, and personal grooming.

We have already touched on wardrobe, so let's chat about accessories.

Accessories are defined as jewelry, eyewear, watches, scarves, ties, belts, hosiery, footwear, handbags, totes, cosmetics, nail color, and visible tattoos.

Accessories are the detailing of a pulled-together look.

ACCESSORY TIPS FOR YOUR PERSONAL STYLE

Earlier, we discussed the five personal style categories. Take a minute to recall what your style category was. Here are some specific tips for each type to consider when accessorizing so you can enhance your style image:

Classic: Timeless and traditional jewelry pieces, which may include a beaded or pearl necklace and earring set. Silk scarves that coordinate with the outfit. Nails that are nude or neutral shades. Solid closed-toed heels with nude hosiery. Leather handbag and/or a structured tote.

Chic: Somewhat classic pieces, yet a bit of modern trend added in the mix. Whatever the color of the season, the chic style has mixed accessories: whether jewelry, a pendant, or a scarf. Shoes are designer, patterned, textured, or multi-colored. The shoe is a statement piece along with her handbag.

Romantic: Finely detailed jewelry which may include dangled pieces, clusters of gems, or hoops. Feminine necklace that is delicate or embellished with gems or flowers. Open-toed strappy shoes, lacy accessories, sheer fabrics, delicate colors, net hosiery. Curved and soft material for a handbag.

Ethnic: Accessories that are comfortable. Possibly smooth or worn leather bands for the necklace and/or bracelet, dangle earrings in earth tones and made of natural fabrics such as feather, leather, or stone. Potential for multiple earrings in one ear, stylish piercings, and unique universal fashions. Soft leather or fabric unstructured handbag.

Dramatic: Bold accessories that make a statement. Geometric or abstract in shape, bold and/or bright in color. Footwear is high-heeled, sleek, and leading the season trend. Handbag is typically large, embellished, and bold like her shoes. If designer, logo is important.

RULE OF 3/10

Rule of 3

Keep in mind odd numbers when styling your jewelry. I understand this can follow the same rule for gardening, hanging pictures, and other areas of visual aesthetic. Here's an example: let's say your fashion style is classic and your accessory choice is pearls. A suggestion would be a pair of pearl earrings, a pearl necklace, and a pearl bracelet. You could substitute the bracelet for a pearl broach. Or, wear them all and add in a fifth pearl item. There is a balanced look when wearing jewelry in odd numbers. You can do the same with any metal pieces too. Play with this and see how it looks on you.

Rule of 10

Without a doubt, the number-one request I get asked from clients is to help them feel confident and look pulled together. They don't want to feel frumpy or invisible. Who would? I think we can all relate to this request at one time or another in our life.

It's truly amazing, but one of the quickest ways to get that "pulled-together look" is to use the "Rule of 10," which is simply counting up the items you have put on your body. All items count as one point with the exception of a pair of earrings: count the pair as one point. If there is a high contrast with a garment piece, count these at two points.

Here's an example. Today, I'm wearing a pair of earrings, necklace, one bracelet, one ring, blouse, black long dress top, black skirt, leggings, boots, and my nails are polished. How many items do you count? Yep, that's 10. Recently, when I was styling at one of my favorite boutiques, I received many compliments on how pulled together I looked.

This concept also explains why another time I had the opposite reaction while doing some personal shopping at a boutique. I had run out of time to do any accessorizing. I caught a glimpse of myself in the mirror and thought, "Why do I look so washed out and frumpy?" Sure enough, I had maybe five items on my body, plus I had not taken the time to put on makeup. Interesting, right? Play with this concept and see what you come up with.

Tip: The exception to this rule is the "dramatic" wardrobe style. A dramatic may have more than 10 items on before she gets halfway down her body.

Let's recap the steps for developing your image and confidence journey:

1) Discover your identifiable personal brand
2) Know your wardrobe style
3) Create a style statement
4) Choose a wardrobe to flatter your unique shape
5) Discover the colors that enhance your eyes, hair, and skin tone
6) Add accessories to build your signature look

In closing, I'd like to share what a blessing it has been for me to get some thoughts on paper and communicate the love I have for helping women feel beautiful. Truly, this love of styling encompasses who I am as an individual. I love my career. It allows me to work with women of all ages, races, sizes, social economic backgrounds, talents, and lifestyles.

I will be the first to raise my hand and say I don't know it all. Every day is a learning opportunity and I embrace the experiences of what I do. My number-one objective in writing this chapter is to give you the framework to build a strong and confident appearance. Here's what this chapter is not. It is not a set of steps to try and change you, shame you, or make you feel unworthy. You, my friend, are worthy, valuable, and beautiful. You are precious.

"Women today are bombarded with conflicting messages of how they should look. When they try to recreate the images they see on TV and magazines they come away frustrated, depressed, and feeling hopeless. My customers love Lisa Fischer for her straightforward, no-nonsense approach to dressing a woman's body shape using the DRES System gems. Once they discover the secrets of body shape and how to make the best of what they thought were flaws, they are immediately empowered with confidence, purpose, and grace."

—Leih Mulvihill (Diamond)

Lisa Fischer
DRES System Certified Personal Stylist
and Director of Education

Renton, Washington
lisajfischer@comcast.net
dressystem.com

Lisa became a Certified Personal Stylist with the DRES System after an exhaustive search to find a premiere training and certification program. There are many certification programs available, yet Lisa chose the DRES System based on its positive and encouraging messaging for her clients.

Lisa is an inspiring leader who offers her clients simplicity, clarity, and practical application whether speaking from stage, talking one-on-one over coffee, or knee-deep in their closet. The DRES System is a stand-alone resource that unites individuals with their best self.

Teaching, listening, and encouraging are just a few of Lisa's strengths when it comes to working with clients. She is a natural communicator who is extremely approachable. Lisa has put her love and passion for teaching to great use as the Director of Education with the DRES System. She consults, trains, and certifies individuals seeking to break into the styling business.

Personal styling, teaching, nurturing brand partnerships, public speaking, and partnering with community fashion shows keep Lisa engaged in what brings her joy and fulfillment.

Lisa is active in the community where she volunteers her time and service to the Business and Professional Women organization as the State Young Careerist Chair, mentoring young professionals between the ages of 21 and 35.

CHAPTER 3

THE POWER OF PERSONAL STYLE

By Giselle Royston

In this chapter you will discover that style goes far beyond fashion and beauty; it is a powerful way to say who you are and get what you want in order to achieve the desires of your heart. Your personal style comes through in a louder voice than anything you might scream from a rooftop. But often, there is so much focus on the outside that you forget to step back and understand that style really starts within. When your outward appearance reflects the best qualities of your personality and talents, there's no limit to what you can achieve!

What Is Style?

What do you think about when you hear someone use the word style? Most commonly, the word style refers to one's fashion or outer appearance. But, I want to remind you that style is much more than your shoulder-length haircut, designer dress, or your Christian Louboutin shoes.

Style is the total combination of the way you dress, talk, and move your body... or anything you do for that matter. Simply put, it's how you express your inner being outwardly. This includes all of your thoughts, emotions, interests, and values. Everything on the outside is merely a reflection of what's on the inside.

Defining style has long preoccupied not just those who don't seem to have it, but also those who are celebrated for it. Style encompasses more than the clothes you wear—what you do and how you do it is just as important. Your personal style shows your uniqueness. The power of style is a subject with endless allure because it can't be neatly defined. In its mystery lies its power. We perceive style instinctively; we know it when we see it.

Fashion vs. Style

Though news and entertainment media usually interchange the terms "fashion" and "style," I do not believe these terms are synonymous. Fashion alone is an external thing, not a way to identify a person. Style, however, is about being whole and balanced. Whether I'm talking about the latest trends or hosting an event, I believe in leading a woman toward discovering her authentic self, her individual personality, and her essence on the inside. Then, she reflects her true self on the outside through style.

Self-Expression Coach

Most people think what I do is simply help people upgrade their outer appearance. This is what they think when they hear "wardrobe consultant" or "personal stylist," and will come to me for a personal shopping session wanting mainly to focus on fashion. I like to think of myself as a "self-expression coach," because I firmly believe that fashion is just one part of style. My makeovers are more about self-discovery and reinvention versus a major transformation.

The most stylish people I know are self-confident, and their clothes reinforce that confidence. I love a hot shoe or a stunning gown as much as the next girl, but style is about a lot more than having a walk-in closet filled to the brim.

Personal style is how you are perceived by others. Do your actions and how you communicate align with your personal style at all times, whether at home, work, or play?

MY STYLE JOURNEY

As a young girl I can remember seeing my mother dressed in her fur coat, gloves, handbags, and matching shoes. She was always dressed well. Dressing up was my mother's way of taking control and making sure she felt her best going into any situation, especially those that left her shaken and scared, though she didn't show it at the time. To her, dressing well was not about vanity, but about respect—for herself and everyone else. I loved playing dress-up in her closet. She was a seamstress; she could take a Vogue pattern and do amazing things with it to create her own designs. She designed my graduation prom gown and coat, which was different from everyone else in my class. I would say that's about the time I developed a respect for style, a love for fashion, and appreciation for fashion as a creative expression.

Lessons Learned

In school, we had a dress code. The girls could wear blouses, skirts, and sweaters—pants were not allowed. We were taught that a student's conduct is related to his/her clothing. When I was in junior high school, all girls in 7th and 8th grade were required to take sewing for half of the year and cooking the other half. The programs were extremely structured. Much later, I took a tailoring class thinking that I would pursue a career in fashion design. What I discovered in my tailoring class was my love for high-quality fabrics. I learned that first and foremost, quality is important because it makes wearing clothes a more enjoyable experience. I learned that the number-one prerequisite to building a great wardrobe is to be able to recognize a quality garment when you see one. This allows you to tell the difference between a durable, well-crafted piece and one that looks pretty on the rack but won't last more than half a season.

I also learned that the distinguishing factors between high-quality and low-quality manufacturers are the extra steps they take to ensure a garment:

1) Looks good after multiple wears and washes
2) Feels comfortable on the skin
3) Is well-fitted. All of these "extras" take time and money

That's why it's so easy to find pretty pieces at budget stores that end up falling apart after a week. To cut costs, the manufacturer focuses on making the garment look good on the hanger instead of its quality. After all, looking good is what brings in sales.

The excitement that comes with wearing a nice skirt, for instance, can be carried over into the way an individual carries herself. My parents used to say "always choose quality over quantity." Turns out they were right because I have a few classic pieces in my wardrobe that have stood the test of time. I can remember when I bought my first "little black dress" almost a decade ago. I couldn't afford it at the time, but I knew it was a great purchase. I ate peanut butter and jelly for a month to pay for it, and that dress still serves me well today. I didn't realize it then, but the cost of the dress was money well spent.

Stylist Startup

I got my start in fashion working as a sales associate at Nordstrom. I challenged myself to be a personal stylist, not a salesperson. I didn't sell pieces, I sold wardrobes. I focused on selling a total look—the dress, the bag, the belt, and the shoes. I was quickly fast-tracked to the personal stylist team. I loved booking my own appointments and working exclusively with clients. I focused on building relationships and establishing trust, and I quickly discovered that was what my clients wanted from me.

I've always wanted to have my own business, so becoming a wardrobe consultant was right up my alley. I love working with people and developing the best look for each and every client. So I decided to take my experience in the fashion and the retail industry to the next level by getting my certification as a Personal Stylist using the DRES System.

Your style is a reflection and a statement to the world about who you are. Everyone has a personal style. I believe that one of the key steps to making the most out of your personal style is to know your body shape and how to dress in a way that complements your best features.

A stylist will help you define and uncover your style potential by eliminating the clutter that distorts who you are. My goal with each client is a complete wardrobe image enhancement, thus creating an empowered you, inside and out.

I believe in leading a woman toward discovering her authentic self, her personality—her essence on the inside—and then reflecting that self on the outside through style.

My goal in this chapter is to help you identify what you'd like others to see, boost your confidence, discover the woman in the mirror, live authentically while aging with grace, and do all of these with style.

DISCOVER THE WOMAN IN THE MIRROR

Do you find yourself agonizing over your reflection in the mirror wondering if what you're wearing looks good on you? I used to ask myself that question every day until I finally realized that seeing myself clearly was more important than what I was wearing.

We would all like to say that when we look in the mirror, the reflection is of a woman who is happy with herself and her life. We want the woman looking back at us to be compassionate and self-assured. Also, you may hope that you're well liked, respected, and personable and that the reflection is a true measure of how others see you. But, are you honest with yourself? Do you take the time to truthfully reflect on who you are as a woman and a human being?

Compassion

I have always found that the most important thing to remember in life (and in business) is this: we're all just people! It doesn't matter what kind of face you put before the public. Forget about judging a book by its cover.

> **Deep down we're all fragile human beings—**
> **each one a combination of victories and defeats,**
> **a mixture of pain, joy, suffering, and hopes.**

Dealing with people is an everyday occurrence. And, while we all need some quiet time to reflect now and then, our interactions with others are probably the most important part of our lives. How you interact with others does more to shape your life, your reputation, and your career than any other single thing you do.

You need to understand that beneath the image you project—the rehearsed smiles and the perfect lines—we are all identical, just people. We are here on this planet to hold each other up and to support one another. Sometimes it seems the challenges in life far outweigh the joys, and that's why we need to be there for each other.

As a self-identified "super-connector" of people, I have always maintained and applied a code of professional etiquette based on the fact that people do business with those they know, trust, and like. In this increasingly impersonalized world of high technology and communication via social media, the key to success is personal consideration. It is important to treat people with respect, be there for them, and conduct yourself with integrity and compassion. How do you "appear" to those you interact with and to those you are meeting for the first time? When I look in the mirror, I see a person who wants to connect with and help people.

Reflections

Here's a question to ponder: What if people don't see in you what *you* see in the mirror? That's why you should always be aware of how you come across to others. If you're not sure, find out. It may be a painful lesson, but it's worth enduring. You'll be better for it. I'll never forget the lesson I learned about myself almost a decade ago—a deep lesson to be sure, but one that will stick with me for a lifetime.

I took a public relations course to strengthen my communication skills. At one point toward the end of the program, we were all asked to pair off with another person. One exercise we did was having the other person act out what they thought about their partner. So, my partner took my purse, flung it across his shoulder, and proceeded to sashay across the room while the three-hundred people in the class witnessed it! His observation was that I was arrogant, aloof, and distant.

I always considered myself a friendly, down-to-earth person so I was really taken aback. Where was his perception of me coming from? I asked a few people in the class what they thought about his impression and they agreed with the assessment. Sometimes friends won't be honest with you about yourself, but strangers will. They pointed out that during our breaks, I would go off by myself and not mingle. The truth is I'm a private person who needs time alone. I get lost in my thoughts. Time alone energizes me and gives me time to think and gain clarity. As a result, I'm able to act with confidence.

Also, I'm an introvert. Everything I do in the outside world causes me to expend energy, after which I need to go back and replenish my spirit in a quiet environment. Spending time on my own allows me to be reflective, and to think about my experiences and reactions to past situations. Had this been a business situation, I would have had no qualms about working the room. But the class wasn't work, and my inhibitions implied to others that I was distant. Perception is reality and we all need to pay attention to how we're perceived.

Sure, my feelings were hurt by the experience. But it was enlightening and important for me to know how people perceived me. Maybe you've been in similar situations or maybe you've perceived something about another person that in reality was way off the mark. We all have different lives shaped by our childhood and all that we experienced growing up.

We're All the Same

I've been blessed with a supportive family, success, and countless good friends, advisors, and mentors. I happened to have worked with a number of well-known people and now through this book I'm becoming an author. My pure intention is to help other women succeed. Because of my accomplishments, I often encounter people who think the person I see in the mirror is better than they are.

Nothing could be further from the truth; I'm no different from anyone else I meet. I have the same personal challenges, doubts, fears, and problems. Once after I gave a speech, a woman came up to me and shared her hope that one day people would want to listen to what she had to say. I thought to myself, "Who in the world would have believed anyone would come and listen to anything I have to say? I'm just Giselle."

I responded, "Girl, I'm no different from you. We're all the same. You can do this, too, and people will want to hear what you have to say."

The truth is you never know what kind of personal baggage someone else is carrying. Yes, people may "look up" to me, but the fact is that I, too, have parts of me I don't like. You may covet some aspect of another person—maybe it's their success, their mate, hair, looks, or possessions. But you must know that the person you are yearning to be like is probably yearning to be like someone else. Be careful what you ask for.

Perceptions or misconceptions can be dangerous and hurtful. If we took the time to just stop and think for a minute, and remind ourselves that we're all human beings, the world would be a better place.

I often think of the story of the grocery store clerk who wrote to advice columnist Ann Landers to complain that she had seen people using food stamps to buy luxury food items like birthday cakes and bags of balloons. She went on to say that she thought all those people on welfare who treated themselves to such non-necessities were lazy and wasteful. But who was she to judge? Who was she to perceive what others may be dealing with? A few weeks later Landers' column was devoted entirely to people who had responded to the grocery clerk.

The ultimate life lesson came from a lady who wrote: "I'm the woman who bought the cake and paid with food stamps. I thought the checkout woman in the store would burn a hole through me with her eyes. What she didn't know (and I would never tell her) is that the cake was for my little girl's birthday. It was her last. She has bone cancer and will probably be gone within six to eight months." Wow, talk about a heartbreaker!

So when you meet someone new, you should always keep in mind that you never know what their background is or what they are personally dealing with at the moment. Nine times out of ten their challenges are the same as yours.

My Truth

As women, we've been faced with our own distinctive struggles and challenges through time. We've built on centuries of misperception, intolerance, and prejudice. But if you work on being honest with yourself and work to become a better human being, the joys outweigh the sorrows. The negative perceptions will fade away, the successes will come your way, and your life, along with the lives of others, will be enriched.

I decided to become an Independent Personal Stylist using the DRES System Certification Course to reconnect with my true self and sense of style. The DRES System has put me in touch with my own body shape, empowered me to feel stylish, smart, and satisfied with a look that's uniquely my own. My continued goal is to pass it on. Now when I look in the mirror, I see a person who has always wanted to help people. I see a woman of substance, a woman of power, a woman of positive influence, and a woman of meaning. I see my truth!

LIVE AUTHENTICALLY

To be who you are truly meant to be is not easy, especially in a world that values what is fake, what is easy, what is quick, and what is on the surface.

Part of your core (and mine) is authenticity. This is the purest and most valuable part of who you are. It is also the most quickly abandoned. The first sign of abandoning your core happens when you are a teenage girl turning into a woman. By the time you became a teenager, you had been stripped of your inner core, you just wanted to fit in and belong. So you became cheerleaders and joined sororities; you hitched your wagon closely to other young women you so desperately wanted to be like. This is our shared plight as women: the struggle to be independent yet interdependent, the need to be an individual but also part of the crowd.

Expectations

Women face immense pressure to conform. We are bombarded with ads and images telling us who we should be as girls and who we should become as women. These campaigns stress what is external versus what is internal. They tell us we are nothing unless we are attractive, thin, and sexy. Let me be clear: being an authentic woman has absolutely nothing to do with any of those things.

Living authentically is not easy, but it is very rewarding. Life is so fragile and you are here for such a short time. So don't waste any of the time you have to give your gifts to the world. Far too many of you have hidden yourselves. You spend your life hiding your true self in order to dance to someone else's music. It is time to learn to live out your power of authenticity.

Be Original

To be authentic is to be an original. It is to be true and not false. It is to be pure, rare, and verifiable. To be authentic means learning to be yourself. And being yourself can be difficult when your core has been rewritten to meet someone else's vision of your life.

A great place to start practicing the art of being authentic is to define what it means to be authentically you.
It is to discover
It is to create
It is to refresh
It is to dance
It is to soar

You must have self-awareness in order to know who you are and what you want from life. Authenticity allows you to connect deeply with others because it requires you to be transparent and vulnerable. Authenticity starts when you set the intention to be genuine.

Happy Inside

So how do you create a life of authenticity? By discovering your life lessons; you wake up one day and you have a courageous conversation with yourself. You stop making what your family, your spouse, and your friends think—or what the world demands—more important than what you think.

You wake up one day and you say, "Enough! I am going to live my life for me before it is over." You make a deal with yourself to release what no longer serves you and to get rid of that which hinders you. You grasp that it is never too late to have a life and never too late to change one. You don't need to be rescued: you need only to be awakened.

It starts by being willing to redefine for yourself what success means, including moving away from traditional standards of what work means, what love means, and what living life means. Being authentic occurs in your heart first. And once you wake up to who you really are and who you are capable of being, life will never be the same. Creating an authentic life that makes you happy starts inside.

One of my clients works for an investment firm in the Bay Area. She was on the fast track. She was dating a very eligible guy with a great career in finance. They were a handsome couple. It seemed that they would have beautiful children and live happily ever after with a big home in the wine country. Right?

Wrong. She did not love him. In fact, I'm not sure she even liked him. He did however fit the script. Yet life has a funny way of giving us a chance to escape the impending prisons we set for ourselves. While preparing to become a partner at work, she started to experience chest pains. It turns out that her heart wasn't the problem; instead she got an unexpected diagnosis, the result of which meant she would never have children. Long story short, he walked away. The irony is, the doctors got it wrong. But the lessons that came from that very difficult period in her life were immense. She needed to see who was authentic in her life.

My point in sharing this story is to say this: my client was headed down a dismal road of conformity to an existence that would have swallowed her whole. She was never meant to live someone else's vision of her life, and neither are you. If she can change her life, you can too!

When you dare to have a real conversation with yourself, all will be well. Not only will it be well, but you will rediscover who you are—the real you the world wants to get to know. How awesome is that?

Being authentic is important to knowing your value. If you know your value, you will embrace your gifts and you will walk in authenticity. Here are several things I have put into practice in my own life, some of which I have adapted from my life coach.

KNOW YOUR VALUE

I will keep repeating this over and over until it catches on. Everything you do as a woman starts with this.

Personal values are your core beliefs, values, and philosophies that you hold about life, its purpose, and your own purpose. As you grow, you take on the personal values of others around you until you reach the teenage years. Then you start to accept or reject such values as being a *part* of who you are, or *not* a part of your true self. Don't just accept the values that were ingrained in you by parents, teachers, and society. You need to stop, take a deep breath, and look at yourself, pinpoint your own values, and implement them into your life.

Choose the values that are most important to you, the values you believe in and define your character. Then live them visibly every day at work and at home. Living your values is one of the most powerful tools available to you to help you be the person you want to be, to help you accomplish your goals and dreams, and to help you lead and influence others. Don't waste your best opportunity.

Face Your Inner Struggles

You cannot live an authentic life with a bunch of conflicts. You have to de-clutter your inside to get to who you are. During this process, reflect upon your dreams, fears, and what motivates you. Ponder why you feel the way you do, and then start working towards overcoming these inner struggles.

Ask the Hard Questions

Ask the people who love you what they see in you. Sometimes you don't see what others can. Ask for help in finding your purpose. And mostly, get still and quiet with yourself so you can hear the answers from within. Here are a few examples of questions I encourage my clients to ask themselves:

Are you happy with yourself?

What is one fear you know is holding you back?

What mistakes do you make over and over again?

DARE TO REDEFINE

It doesn't matter if you are twenty or sixty, it is never too late to be who you might have been. But you cannot get there if you don't have the courage to make changes.

- **Put your goals in writing.** The act of writing down what you are going to do is a strong motivator. Writing down goals prevents you from leaving them vague. Be specific.
- **Make a list of obstacles.** Think of everything that might stand in your way. Then, decide what you can do about each obstacle. Design a plan to reduce the influence of each obstacle and increase the chances that you will be successful in reaching your goal.
- **List the benefits of achieving your goal.** Knowing exactly what you will gain from reaching your goal is a strong motivator. For example, keeping your checkbook balanced will give you more spending money on the weekends. Walking a mile every morning will help you to stay focused at work.

Trust Your Instincts

Of all I have learned in my sixty-something years of living, among the most important is to trust my intuition and instincts. This is your authentic-self communicating with your false-self. You need to listen to that voice inside of you which is speaking the truth and follow through on what it tells you.

Connect With People Who Share Your Value

You have to run with other authentic people. If you spend time with shallow, masked people, you will become one. Surround yourself with people who are transparent, honest, and authentic.

AGE GRACEFULLY

To age is a gift. To age is to become wise and to share the great light radiating from within you. To age is to be fearless, to mature, and to grow more compassionate, more loving, and more complete.

To age gracefully is to share what you've learned from your failures and your successes. You accept aging as a part of living. You accept that your face may change, your hair may grow thinner and grayer, your body will wrinkle, and frown lines may appear on your face.

One of the greatest things about being a woman is that (although we may operate by the same life values as our mothers and grandmothers) when it comes to our values and aging gracefully, I think we have learned a new way of embracing the life cycle as women.

The Journey

Finding your way through this process is not easy. Yet, with each passing year, you learn to embrace each moment. You begin to appreciate the wonder and awe of life and the preciousness of what it means to be alive. You accept that the small aches will come and that you won't move as fast as you once did. It's okay, because if you are aging, you are living! If you're under thirty, please do not pass this over or think it doesn't apply to you. Just keep living and I promise you with all my heart that someday this section will apply to you.

Everybody has heard the common saying that sixty is the new fifty, but what does that really look like when having to face it? Yes, you can exercise and do all the things to keep your body fit, but you can't avoid the aging process. How you decide to deal with it will create either a rich and rewarding journey or a painful one. If there is one thing that women universally fear, it is the aging process. Youth is celebrated, elevated, and adored. Beauty is skinny, sleek, and tall. Lush hair of varying lengths is what you worship. You are conditioned from the time you are little girls to want to be beautiful. So when you are not, you are devastated. You do all manner of things to become and stay young and beautiful, often at the expense of your own self-worth and value.

Face Yourself

Guess what? You no longer have to fear aging. Yes, you will lose some things when you age. But you will also gain so much more perspective, joy, confidence, courage, self-love, assurance, peace, deeper connection with those you love, and freedom. I am going to share with you the four strategies for aging gracefully with the goal of helping you to embrace each area, encourage others, and become a better woman at every turn. I want to help you to age gracefully. Not just on the outside, but on the inside where it really matters. All of us have met someone who radiates light just beneath the surface of their eyes and their wrinkles; often they are little old ladies who light up when they see other people or their great grandchildren. These women live long because they face themselves early in life, get rid of needless distractions and life stressors, and run full throttle at life.

The life cycle of being born, living, and ultimately dying is a process of aging. The most significant thing any woman (young or old) can do to unlock the secrets of aging gracefully is to start with acceptance. You will age. Period. So lean into it, make fun of it, and have fun with it. How many of us have lost girlfriends in their thirties, forties, and fifties to breast cancer, heart disease, or other ailments? To be alive is a gift. When life may not be going well, remember that if you woke up this morning you got a second chance to live well. Do something, experience something on your bucket list, say "I love you" or "Will you forgive me?" one more time. Each new day brings with it an opportunity to begin again. It's a fresh start every 24 hours.

Confident Woman

The problem is that many women who are over fifty spend all of their time trying to look young, be hot, and be chic instead of being themselves. I interviewed a few young men who told me that there is nothing worse than a middle-aged or aging woman who is not comfortable in her own skin, running around in short dresses, super high heels, and clothing that trends younger. In fact, many of those men said they much prefer an attractive, confident, older woman in every way as opposed to being with a younger, beautiful twenty-something who doesn't know who she is or what she wants from life.

Confidence, then, is an important virtue that will help you as you age. It's like a magnet to men at work, in the dating game, and in a marriage. Confident women are not to be confused with aggressive, overworked, stressed-out know-it-alls. These qualities tend to be turn-offs to men. But as you age, you will come into yourself. An old boyfriend's mother once told me, "Giselle, one day you will get comfortable with yourself and that will be a great day in your life." I did not understand what she meant then, but I most certainly do now.

Acceptance is freedom. It allows you to move past your regrets, your mistakes, and your fears. Acceptance allows you to deal with what is and what can still be, and put to rest what is lost. Age comes in seasons. We are children, then teens, and before you know it young adults. Our twenties blow by, and our thirties are ever so busy. Then our forties arrive and you begin looking back to see what you've missed instead of taking hold of what you still have ahead. Aging is not what it was in the 1800s, and 1900s. Aging women of the 21st Century look fit and healthy (without plastic surgery) well into their sixties and beyond. As they say, sixty really is the new fifty!

I interviewed dozens of cross-generational women, from all walks of life, ages twenty to ninety-five, to discover themes about how to embrace aging gracefully. I asked them to share their tips, such as beauty secrets, daily facial/body regimes, special anti-aging ingredients, routine dietary tips, people they spent their time with, family secrets, love secrets, or life secrets. Here are the four strategies of aging gracefully that were shared with me which I now practice in my own life.

1) Take Care of Your Physical Body and Appearance

I have used a skincare regime as long as I can remember. And I have to admit being faithful to a daily cleansing, moisturizing, and toning routine has worked wonders. But let's be honest, your ethnic background, gene pool, and where you live all play a part in how well you are physically. Important practices are staying out of the sun, drinking lots of water, moisturizing your skin, taking vitamins and calcium, engaging in weight-bearing exercises, keeping your BMI at a normal level, and eliminating white sugar and flour from your diet; these are the obvious things we all know to do.

A good rule of thumb is, if you aren't a teenager, don't dress like one. You also have to wear less makeup as you age, and keep it fresh, clean, and classic. Consider wearing short, chic hair versus long hair. Short hair accentuates the facial features. Long hair as you age tends to pull the face down. And watch those highlights. As you age, lighter (or gray) hair tends to wash you out.

The goal then is to take good care of your physical body so you can look better, but not necessarily younger. Be mindful of weight gain or loss that begins to creep up on you. Tend to aging spots. Get sleep because it is critical to your wellness as a woman. Your looks depend a lot on your physical routine, so stay busy.

Various medical resources and research studies say that there are five important principles, among many, to aging well:

1) Being married—married people live longer and age better

2) Having a healthy love and sex life

3) Experiencing lots of laughter

4) Drinking green tea, black tea, and, believe it or not, red wine. They are all super rich in antioxidants that doctors and scientists agree help with lessening the chances of getting cancer, heart disease, and Alzheimer's disease

5) Taking care of your teeth and gums—consider whitening your teeth to renew your youthful smile

2) Take Care of Your Emotional Well-Being

Acknowledging how you feel is important as you age. Whether you journal it, form book clubs where you can discuss it, or just share with close friends, acknowledging where you are on life's journey gives you a healthy perspective and possible solutions to deal with aging. It's okay to have some feelings about the fact that you will not always be the youngest, prettiest woman in the room.

My mother said, "Complaining and whining are not good for you, they create negative energy. Your attitude determines a lot about how you will look in this life."

3) Take Care of Your Spiritual Health

I talked earlier about possessing a light that radiates from within your soul regardless of your age. It is your spirit that people either love or hate. A woman may not have a supermodel's look, but I have seen many a woman land a handsome prince because she had a light that draws men. She radiates peace, calm, and compassion.

Your faith is another key component in how you age through the seasons of your life. Make time for exercise, meditation, prayer, naps, short breaks, relaxing music, walks at lunchtime, connection with nature, and spiritual things. Tap into your creativity. Having a good life balance allows you to tap into your right brain—the calmer, more powerful, and artistic you.

4) Maintain Healthy Relationships

Last, and in my opinion the ultimate key to aging well, is to have good lifelong friendships and connections that serve as your support network. There are well-documented, proven health benefits of being close to your family, friends, and colleagues, and of attending social events.

Do not be alone for long periods of time; get out and do things. It is also important to have continuity and consistency in your relationships. Keep people around who know your history and who can be trusted. Most important, be open to having younger friendships and connections. Look for the new, good, and interesting things in life. Embrace that love can come again, even in your later years.

The great secret to aging gracefully is this: the core of who you are doesn't change. Your body does, but you are the same in many ways that count. So stay young inside. Say good things, practice compassion, and have peaceful, loyal, loving people in your life who bring those virtues to your private space. Live in the present. You need something to look forward to and to chase. Don't obsess over what you can no longer do. Focus on what you can *still* do. Just do it with style.

Aging Gracefully Secret

As I said in the introduction, style goes far beyond fashion and beauty; it is a powerful way to say who you are and get what you want in order to achieve the desires of your heart.

Most important, remember that your true power of style is extremely personal and constantly evolving. It's a fluid process of self-discovery, influenced by your situations as well as your personal evolution. Similar to your taste in foods, your favorite types of music, and the television shows you watch on a regular basis, your style sensibilities will change over the years. I don't know about you, but I'm a much different person today than I was ten, fifteen, and twenty years ago. So remember that discovering your style is a journey, not a destination.

"Giselle's four-step process on aging gracefully is brilliant. Her care and love for her reader shines throughout each tip, story, and message. I smiled, felt inspired, and had tears brought to my eyes while reading her message."

—Nikki Rausch (Sapphire)

Giselle Royston
DRES System Certified Personal Stylist

Bellevue, Washington
giselleroyston@gmail.com
dressystem.com

Giselle Royston, Personal Stylist, has been teaching women and men how to develop and maintain their authentic style for over ten years. Tapping into each client's individual potential, Giselle guides her clients through a unique styling system that helps them discover how to put their "best look forward." Through years of retail experience, Giselle has discovered that looking your personal best directly relates to a positive self-image and strong self-confidence.

Giselle transitioned from a successful retail career, including working for Nordstrom, Neiman Marcus, and Eileen Fisher, to being a consultant. Her lifetime goal has always been to have her own business, so becoming a consultant is right up her alley. Her personal relationship approach has afforded her the opportunity to work with hundreds of clients over the years.

As an Independent Personal Stylist using the DRES System Certification Course, Giselle has built a strong portfolio of clients spanning all ages, income levels, and seasons of life. She believes "beauty is about being comfortable in your own skin and knowing and accepting who you are." Empowering her clients to reach their goals, dreams, and ambitions is her greatest passion.

Giselle received the 2014 Emerging Business Owner of the Year award from *Eastside Women in Business*. She is chair of the procurement committee for Olive Crest–Western Washington, a non-profit organization dedicated to preventing child abuse, to treating and educating at-risk children, and to preserving the family "one life at a time." She is actively involved with the National Association of Women MBAs, and is passionate about higher education, and increased leadership roles for women.

In her spare time, Giselle enjoys reading, as well as domestic and international travel where she has had the opportunity to visit some of the world's finest wineries.

She has two adult sons and lives in Bellevue, Washington, with her husband.

CHAPTER 4

REINVENTING YOURSELF

By Mary Angelosante

Benjamin Franklin said, "There are only two things that are certain in life: death and taxes." I would like to add to that supposition, that another thing certain in life is change. As a former military wife of twenty-six years and as a middle-aged woman, I know this to be true. And I am sure if you think about it, the same is true for you, too. In our lifetimes, the pace of change has increased exponentially. As I was growing up, we had no computers or cell phones; thus the computer and technological age has changed life as I knew it. The churning of events and discoveries made in our lifetime causes some uncertainty and makes us wonder how we fit into this ever-changing whirlwind of life. How do you define and present yourself to the world?

Reinvention Process

In this chapter, I will write about the process of reinventing yourself. In so doing, I have come up with four steps to bring about a reinvention.

1) Accept that change is inevitable and necessary
2) Understand and formulate your personal identity
3) Take action to know yourself
4) Increase your self-confidence

I'll share some examples and insights I learned about taking these steps along the way as a military wife. I include some quotes from very wise, well-known people that illustrate my points. These quotes eloquently and simply sum up what I feel and are reflected in the examples I provide in this chapter. I will also give an example about how color analysis and the principles of the DRES System helped me earlier in life and how they have helped me again recently as I have embarked on my most recent reinvention. I believe so strongly in the principles of the DRES System that I have become a DRES Personal Stylist myself. What has helped me so much in my life can help you, too!

Moving made me reinvent my life with each change of location. While in the military, we moved seventeen times in twenty-six years. Hopefully by reading about snippets of my life you will be able to relate it to your own unique story. Warren G. Bennis, states, "People who cannot invent and reinvent themselves must be content with borrowed postures, secondhand ideas, fitting in instead of standing out." I couldn't agree more with Bennis' quote.

Significance

Most people would rather pilot their own ship than take a back seat. Innately, people want to stand out, be noticed, be recognized, and feel important. It is almost second nature to want some sort of control over your life.

Another quote that resonates on the subject of reinvention is from the renowned author, C.S. Lewis. He says,

> **"It may be hard for an egg to turn into a bird; it would be a jolly sight harder for it to learn to fly while remaining an egg. We are like eggs at present, and you cannot go on indefinitely being just an ordinary, decent egg. We must be hatched or go bad."**

This quote speaks to the fact that we all have a destiny to fulfill. If we don't at least try, we will remain an egg filled with endless unutilized potential. We all have a desire to become extraordinary in some way so that we have significance.

ACCEPT THAT CHANGE IS INEVITABLE AND NECESSARY

The question for us all is, How do we acknowledge and cope with change and how do we reinvent ourselves when the need arises, which it inevitably will? When we stop to think about it, from the moment of our birth our life changes, sometimes daily. We can extrapolate that change is just a normal part of life. For some people, change comes more easily, while for others, it is a little more challenging. Earlier in my life, I found the latter to be true for me. Change was uncomfortable. For many people, including me, it is our nature to resist change. It is easier to stick with the familiar. We find it easy to form habits which we are good at following, and then feel more comfortable coasting along in our entrenched way of going about our lives. There is a confidence in, and a feeling of mastery about, our lives in familiar territory.

Then there is that ever-present fear of failure that exists to prevent us from going out on a limb too often.

"Go out on the limb—that is where the fruit is."

—H. Jackson Brown Jr.

In other words, nothing ventured, nothing gained. The sweetest things in life are attained by going above and beyond and taking risks.

With age and experience, we learn that no matter how resistant we are to change, change happens. So it makes good sense to accept it and make the most of it. It is even possible to thrive when change occurs. Resistance takes a back seat to being more open to all the possibilities, which adds another dimension to life. Change can really bring about excitement and anticipation if we allow it to. Keeping an open mind and trying to remain flexible instead of rigid determination to stay the same, no matter what, is helpful and wise.

No Regrets

After you come to the conclusion that change is inevitable and learn to accept it, then you can come to the point of embracing it. The famed author, Mark Twain, put it this way, "Twenty years from now you will be disappointed by the things you didn't do rather than by the ones you did. So throw off the bowlines. Sail away from the safe harbor. Catch the trade winds in your sails. Explore, Dream, Discover." In other words, what will you regret *not* having done? This is encouragement to just "go for it." Jump in with both feet and reap the benefits that change can bring. Maybe for the long-term it is good to have a bucket list of goals you want to achieve, which gives you a roadmap or a plan to follow. I have heard it more than once, if you don't plan to succeed, you plan to fail.

THE MILITARY WIFE

In early adulthood, I was introduced to change and reinvention. It was a change that affected me throughout my life. As I remember, it was a sink or swim moment. Imagine jumping off a cliff, not knowing where you will land or even, for that matter, how you will survive. That is how I felt when I was twenty-three and newly married to an Army officer who was sent to Germany on his first assignment after our wedding. I was young and inexperienced when it came to travelling out of the country. While it is very common for young people to travel outside the country today, it was not in 1982. I was confident about life as I knew it up to that point, but not beyond what I had experienced. Suffice it to say, the identity I worked hard to create entered a state of transition.

My husband of seven months left for Germany in June. Initially, I was prepared to be separated for three to six months waiting for housing which was not a fun thought, but at least I would have time to prepare myself for the long journey ahead. I stayed with my parents in Coeur d'Alene, Idaho, until I could join my husband. To my delight and surprise, I got word that we had housing and I would be able to join Jim in Germany after just three weeks! Almost in the next breath, I began to realize that I was going on a thirteen-hour flight out of the country, with no more than I could pack in my suitcases…by myself. I would leave everything that was familiar to me—my job, my family, my two Siamese cats, and a country where speaking English was the norm.

Solitude

Had this all happened later in my life I would have realized and appreciated it as a tremendous opportunity and I would have envisioned what a grand adventure it could be. Instead, because of my unsureness and lack of experience, it began what would be one of the greatest challenges of my life. I left the comforts of home and all that was familiar and reassuring for a life I no longer recognized as my own. I had been a student for the largest share of my life and had recently become a registered nurse. I had only worked five months when we were assigned to Germany. My husband, Jim, was a First Lieutenant in the Army, an Air Defense Artilleryman, and had begun a career that would place many demands upon him, including being gone a lot. This was during the Cold War and he was serving in Europe on a NATO mission. I spent many lonely hours by myself.

Terrorism was just beginning to occur near where we lived. Looking back on it is quite scary, although at the time we weren't overly concerned about it. Initially, I lived upstairs from a German couple. We did our best to communicate as I knew very little German and they spoke little English. I took a conversational German class meant to be an introduction to help me acclimate to this new world. My landlords were great people who tried to make me feel at home and brought me German treats to eat occasionally.

Flexibility

Prior to going to Germany, I had always imagined I would be working in a hospital utilizing the degree I had worked so hard to earn. Reality hit hard a second time when I realized that if I chose to work (which required rotating shifts) I would be gone many of the times Jim would be home. Also I would have an hour drive to the US Army hospital driving on the Autobahn, which is the German equivalent of a freeway...with no speed limit. All those masterfully engineered German cars built for speed zip by regardless of the weather. To top it off, it was fall and very foggy, and I wasn't that familiar with the road or confident reading German signs. Consequently, I elected not to work in nursing at that time.

"All great changes are preceded by chaos."

—Deepak Chopra

I didn't yet know how much this quote would apply to me in my life. In choosing not to work in nursing, I eliminated one of the parts of my identity that I was sure of, and simultaneously threw myself into personal chaos.

UNDERSTAND AND FORMULATE YOUR PERSONAL IDENTITY

It would be safe to say that as a result of my new marriage and a move out of the country where I could not communicate easily, I began having an identity crisis. For me this manifested itself with increasing anxiety during a time of personal identity adjustment. Because of the changes in my personal circumstances and because I chose not to work in the career I had prepared for, I needed to redefine my own identity. Personal identity is what defines you: it's your uniqueness in the world. In developing a personal identity, several influences come into play. These include genetics, personality style, environmental or societal influences, and personal choice.

GENETICS

As a mother of two beautiful daughters, I became aware that there is a genetic predisposition to personality that shows up very early on in life. My older daughter, Jennifer, was very curious and able to concentrate from the age of six weeks on. She would listen intently and watch the pictures in books I would read to her. She could sit for hours and read books with my help. As Jennifer got a little older, she was very compliant and listened to me if I asked her not to touch something. On the other hand, one of my friends had a daughter who just couldn't sit still to look at books. Her daughter was more active and liked to explore her environment from the start. She tested the boundaries and was always getting into something she wasn't supposed to.

My younger daughter, Dawn, was more outgoing than her sister when they were children. She would often have to hold her older sister's hand and coax her to follow because Jennifer was more hesitant to venture out than her younger sister. It was clear early on that my daughters had different personalities.

We have all heard of the comparisons of opposing personality types. One person may be an extrovert while another is an introvert. One person is optimistic while another is pessimistic. It is generally accepted that those personality traits have a genetic tendency. In other words, specific traits are programmed into an individual's genetic code. I found this to be true watching my two infant daughters. They just seemed to be born with personality traits right from the start that were noticeable before they had a chance to "learn them."

PERSONALITY STYLE

Personality style is a large and very influential part of your personal identity. In the book *The New Personality Self-Portrait*, John M. Oldham and Lois B. Morris state that "Your personality style is your organizing principle. It propels you on your life path. It represents the orderly arrangement of all your attributes, thoughts, feelings, attitudes, behaviors, and coping mechanisms. It is a distinctive pattern of your psychological functioning—the way you think, feel, and behave—

that makes you definitely you. You do of course, grow and change throughout your lifetime, but you do so in a consistent, characteristic manner. Your personality style is your way of being, of becoming, and meeting life's challenges."

Having knowledge about how influential personality style is frees you from feeling you "should" be like your best friend, or anyone else for that matter, because clearly you are you. In my early years, I wrongly assumed everyone thought like me. It is good to remind ourselves of the fact that we are programmed differently from one another. Life would truly be boring if we were all exactly alike.

ENVIRONMENTAL OR SOCIETAL INFLUENCES

These include trends that are popular at a given time, or norms that society seems to embrace. Smoking was common at one time in this country. Many people smoked because it was the "in thing to do." The consequences were not known. Now, it is less popular because we know there are long-term health consequences associated with smoking.

Another example of environmental influences might be parenting styles. Over the years, parenting styles have changed with new ideas about childrearing. When I was a child, it was uncommon to give kids a choice about what to eat. Children ate what was put in front of them without any say whatsoever about it. When my children were young (much to my grandmother's horror) I gave them choices about what they would like to eat.

Changes in style and seasonal colors also represent environmental influences. Designers dictate, to some extent, what fashions and colors will be popular in a given year. I have found that to be one of the biggest challenges in dressing; resisting styles that don't fit my fashion personality. I have had more than one item of clothing in my closet that sits unworn because I chose to ignore my own style and buy something trendy, but out of my comfort zone. Designers influence colors that are "popular" as seasons change, too. Resisting new colors if they are not flattering is best as they steal from your natural beauty.

PERSONAL CHOICE

An important part of identity is influenced by personal choice. People can choose how they define and present themselves to the world. In sharing some of the insights I gained all those years ago when I was a newlywed living far from home, I highlight the fact that little by little, I began giving up some of the things that had defined me. Most notable at the time was the loss of my professional identity as a nurse. That caused a cascading loss of identity, my sense of self. I lost what confidence I did have because I was faced with changing circumstances and had not yet regained a level of self-confidence or self-awareness. I had no close friends or relatives to talk with on a regular basis and at that time there were no computers.

I communicated with my family and friends by mail or cassette tape recordings that could take several weeks or more to arrive. It was so costly to phone home that calls were reserved only for emergencies. After eight months, we moved into military housing at the military base. Up until that time, I felt very isolated and alone many days, and felt a total lack of control over my life. Once we moved on post, I had more chances to meet other military wives who were in the same situation I was in. I made some good friends and had people to talk to again. Despite all of this, I hit rock bottom. But thanks to the love and support of my family and one very special nursing friend I had made, I ever so slowly began to pick myself up, and tried to make sense of how I fit into this new world I was a part of.

"Getting over a painful experience is like crossing the monkey bars. You have to let go at some point in order to move forward."

—C.S. Lewis

I had to let go of the life I knew previously and accept the fact that I was no longer a student and that I chose not to work varying shifts required in the hospital. I would have to learn to speak some German to enhance my living situation. In other words, I had to accept that the negatives that seemed like roadblocks were helping me to learn, and the new normal was not bad—just different. I could adapt my life to this new reality. I would begin to formulate a new identity.

How exactly do you create a new identity? I began reading self-help books.

I learned a lot of helpful insights about myself that enabled me to change my feelings of having no control over my life. I also realized I had all the control I needed (within the parameters of military life) to modify myself in my new circumstances. I had to stop thinking about what I couldn't do and concentrate on what I *could* do. I opened myself up to the possibilities.

TAKE ACTION TO KNOW YOURSELF

Once you discover your personal identity by examining your genetics, personality style, environmental or societal influences, and personal choices, you build a foundation for yourself. This foundation can be built upon or remodeled. This is an ongoing process and a journey. It is so crucial to be who you are; a person unique in the world. No other person has your exact eye, hair, or skin color. You have strengths, weaknesses, and passions. It is so easy to compare yourself to others you believe are prettier or funnier or smarter. You can easily see the beauty and uniqueness in others and yet, somehow, the ability to see those things in yourself eludes you.

Your Spirit

You were born blessed with special gifts and abilities. They may be hard to recognize or accept at times throughout your life, but the Bible even validates our specialness. 1 Corinthians 12: 7–11 says: "Now to each one the manifestation of the Spirit is given for the common good. To one there is given through the Spirit the message of wisdom, to another the message of knowledge by the means of the same Spirit, to another faith by the same Spirit, to another gifts of healing by that one Spirit, to another miraculous powers, to another prophecy, to another distinguishing between spirits, to another speaking indifferent kinds of tongues, and still to another the interpretation of tongues. All these are the work of one and the same Spirit, and he gives them to each one, just as he determines."

In other words, each of us has certain God-given talents that come natural to us or that we choose to master. We're meant to help and serve others. That is a very awesome and profound thought. Many times we have the feeling that we are small and insignificant but we each have a defined purpose or gift to use for the betterment of us all.

Your Personality

It is important to define yourself so you can confidently present a clear picture of who you are to the world. It does take thought and introspection, but it is well worth the effort. One thing that helped me immensely to know and understand myself was taking the Myers-Briggs Type Indicator test. Isabel Briggs Myers and her mother, Katharine Cook Briggs, began creating the indicator during World War II to help women who were entering the workforce for the first time to identify the sort of wartime jobs that they would be best suited for. Their work is just as relevant today and has been used extensively in many companies and workplaces.

There are workshops that specialize in this testing, numerous versions online, or you can read the book *Please Understand Me*, which utilizes the principles of the Myers-Briggs testing. In that book, David Keirsey and Marilyn Bates write about character and temperament types. They say, "People are different in fundamental ways. They want different things: they have different motives, purposes, aims, values, needs, drives, impulses, urges. Nothing is more fundamental than that. They believe differently: they think, cognize, conceptualize, perceive, understand, comprehend, and cogitate differently." The book is a resource to discover exactly what makes you "tick." It also sheds light on what makes others "tick" which should help illuminate and celebrate our differences.

Sometimes friends or relatives who are the closest to you can help you see the traits, abilities, or talents you possess, more clearly than you can see them. A good thing to do is just open a discussion with them about what they see as your strengths and weaknesses. You may be very surprised at the insights they have.

Your Best Self

Hindsight is 20/20, and there is so much I wish I would have known about life in my early twenties that has taken a lifetime to learn. I now appreciate that those scary, lonely days in Germany became important life lessons that had me dig deep—to struggle, explore, and force me to grow as a person. It wasn't easy and it was a real test of mental fortitude, but I wouldn't trade it for the world. Now I realize and appreciate that this was my journey to begin discovering and defining who I was in my adult life. It seemed like it was an excruciatingly slow and arduous process, but little by little I learned that one can truly bloom wherever they are planted. Realizing this was important, because military life required me to move often and I really wanted to be my "best self" wherever I relocated.

TAKING ACTION

Another thing I did for myself, all those years ago in Germany when I lost my sense of my own identity due to major changes in my life, was to have my colors analyzed. I had always been interested in dressing nicely—and I loved sewing and creating any kind of art I could for fun and entertainment. I also loved to decorate my home. Those activities became my hobbies. What I discovered (by mistake almost) was that I felt better about myself when I put on an outfit I felt good in. When I wore something that fit me well or was a beautiful flattering color, I could tell I had more confidence. I also felt better when I took the time, even if I did not feel like it, to put on makeup. Somehow, wearing nice clothes and taking the time to apply makeup made me matter to me.

Intro to Color

At an Army wives' club function, we had a demonstration of the color analysis that was popular at the time, which included a determination of your fashion style. I signed up to do an individual consultation. It was so much fun and I was convinced that the concept of people looking their best in certain colors was true. I discovered that my fashion style was "classic romantic." I had my colors analyzed ten years later just for fun and got the same results. I was convinced I was a "cool" person and I wore only "cool" colors, which I felt at the time were the most flattering colors on me. My fashion style remained the same, too. I realize looking back that dressing with intention, in a way that was flattering to me, gave me a sense of myself again. I had my own identity that was unique, and my own style that reflected my fashion personality. It gave me a kind of confidence that bled over into other parts of my life. I had a sense of control over my life again. I was feeling good because I knew who I was. I had begun to create a new identity for myself simply by what I wore. It sounds very simplistic, but knowing the best colors and style for me had a huge influence in how I felt about everything else in my life.

Dress-Up

A fun activity that may help you define your fashion style is to cut out pictures from magazines of clothing you like or home interiors you prefer. Do you choose more traditional looks or more modern?

I remember back to my early childhood, when my sister and I used to have a big trunk of dress-up clothes that we loved to play with. Back then, we felt like little princesses when we put on those pretty dresses and high heels. I guess what began as a simple truth so early in our childhoods could be a truth for adulthood as well. We feel better when we feel pretty. Somehow though, almost as inevitably, as we make other changes in our lives, doubts surface, and we seem to forget or become unsure about the simple fact that feeling pretty and put together is important for us. Doing so makes us feel better about everything else in our lives. We feel like we are competent, in control, and ready to take on the world.

INCREASE YOUR SELF-CONFIDENCE

Once a person takes the time to know and define themselves, it is a natural consequence to gain, regain, or reestablish self-confidence—the firm belief in yourself and your abilities. It is so important to gain self-confidence because without it you feel like your house is built on shaky ground.

Self-confidence is developed over time with much thought and refinement. It happens as you mature like a fine wine.

Maturity is being fully developed in mind and body. Normal aging and moving through the different stages of life contribute to the complexities of a person's being like the layers of petals on a beautiful flower. As you mature, it becomes easier to accept your gifts and talents without being as critical of yourself as you were when you were younger.

Adapt

Self-confidence also seems to come from living life and adapting to its changing circumstances. It becomes easier to embrace change instead of resisting it with every part of your being. Change becomes easier once you have had previous success with it. With multiple changes and successes, change becomes even easier. You can't help but be moved by the cumulative experiences of life which help shape and define you and give you self-confidence.

Evaluate

Periodic reevaluation can also lead to more self-confidence. You have the option to keep the characteristics you develop over time or discard the characteristics you are no longer happy with or that no longer suit you. For example, a pessimistic person can learn to become optimistic by changing thought patterns. Wisdom comes with age and the ability to more easily know and feel confident about yourself. Adaptation is also a normal part of maturing and internalizing what you learn along the way.

"To exist is to change, to change is to mature, to mature is to go on creating oneself endlessly."

—Henri Bergson

I find great clarity in Bergson's observation. In some ways, it would be boring to remain exactly the same for the entirety of our lives. Instead, we get to have experiences and opportunities to learn from, which may affect us and cause us to modify, change, or reinvent ourselves. That may be the essence of life in a nutshell. It is like the caterpillar spinning a cocoon and becoming reborn as a beautiful butterfly.

Being a military wife, there were times when I was in a position to be a leader, or a role model to wives who were younger. Early on, I had to fake it sometimes, because I lacked confidence and experience. Over time though, with lots of practice, I developed both abilities.

Change

Another part of military life was moving frequently. Believe it or not, many military people moved more than seventeen times in their careers! Part of moving frequently is the need to move light. In other words, we didn't want to move anything that wasn't being used. We found that the more we could be organized, the less stress we would feel. We made moving fun by making it into an adventure. We got new fun travel gear like crayons, color books, sticker books, magazines, and new CDs to sing with in the car. We sang at the top of our lungs as we traversed the country en route to our new homes. We tried to remove some of the sting of leaving good friends that we had made, by starting over in some ways.

My two daughters, Jennifer and Dawn, would get to redecorate their rooms when we got to the new place so they could feel a sense of control over their lives. They were artistic and creative and reveled in the experience. I, too, enjoyed making each new house a home. I learned a lot about decorating and making do with furnishings we already had. It became a puzzle challenge to get all the pieces to fit. We took our beloved cats, Mimi and Mischief, with us wherever we moved, too, which gave us all a sense of continuity. We were blessed to make new friends at each new location who became part of our family in many ways as we were all far away from our own families.

REINVENTION

All the "life lessons" you experience throughout life prepares you to reinvent yourself when the need arises. Inevitably though, once you reach a state of self-confidence or equilibrium, something will change that requires another adaptation or reinvention. It could be a change in life circumstances like getting married, having a baby, getting a promotion, or moving to a new location and climate.

Sometimes what causes change or a need for reinvention is some kind of adversity like a divorce or losing a job. Other times, reinvention is needed due to boredom or feeling stuck in a rut and not fully living up to your potential. "Never too old, never too bad, never too late, never too sick to start from scratch once again," is how Bikram Choudhury sees it. I do believe this to be true, too. As long as we are living, we are changing, if nothing more than advancing through the various stages of life.

"Sometimes you have to let everything go—purge yourself. If you are unhappy with anything—whatever is bringing you down—get rid of it. Because you will find that when you are free, your true creativity, your true self comes out."

—Tina Turner

Identity

When my youngest daughter was a junior in high school, I went back to the nursing career that I had started so many years before. Nursing was an ideal career for me, a very good fit, rewarding and fulfilling. I learned along the way that often patients just need to talk with someone who will listen and be an objective observer. In other words, people want to feel validated and noticed—that they matter in this world. Having my nursing job gave me a strong sense of identity which I so value. I worked at the same office for twelve years, which was a real blessing, and then I decided to make a big change and try something new just to shake things up a bit. After all, I had moved and changed often in my past.

Once again my life called upon me to get uncomfortable, leave the past behind, and forge a new trail. I found that even with years of practice, I began to question myself and parts of my identity.

By accident one day, I went to a Chico's women's clothing store after a phone invitation from the Chico's staff to look at some new fashions. Coincidentally, a DRES Stylist was there giving helpful tips on body shapes and doing a quick color analysis for the women who attended. Like years before, I was interested in color. I had been noticing that the colors I had been wearing didn't seem to look good on me anymore, I thought it might be my hair color, but reasoned that my hair color hadn't changed that much. To me, my skin color hadn't changed that much either. I just felt disconnected from myself and I wasn't sure how to correct that because I had my colors analyzed twice in the past as "cool," so I adhered rigidly to that idea for thirty-plus years. After being told by the DRES Stylist that I was "warm," I knew I had to pursue that proclamation further.

Alignment

I did not believe it at first, because more than anything, in the back of my mind, I was thinking about my closet at home full of cool-colored clothing and how I had spent a lot of money buying those clothes. But, I had to admit to myself that gold looked much better on me than silver and I realized this had everything to do with the disconnect I was feeling with myself. I scheduled a consultation with my DRES Stylist, and basically signed up for all the different services DRES offers. I was curious and I realized that wearing complementary colors could change the way I felt about myself. I remembered how this had helped me back in Germany when I was going through a life transition. In case you are wondering, yes, I did end up buying new clothes that look more flattering on me. I feel like a totally new person in more ways than one. I got to live the first part of my life wearing "cool" colors and I will spend the second part of my life wearing "warm" colors. That is part of the spice of life. My whole family can tell you that I previously wouldn't look at anything orange. Now it is one of my best colors. I even splurged on a stylish orange coat!

Discovery

After working with the stylist, I realized I was at a crossroads. I was trying to organize and simplify my life, looking for a new job or career, and forging a new or modified, updated, and reinvented existence. Once again, the principles I had learned so long ago about being confident in style and being true to myself resurfaced. It was empowering. It came to me almost like a lightning bolt: that I would thoroughly enjoy becoming a DRES Stylist myself. I had always loved clothes, jewelry, and accessories. I understood that there really is a science behind the fact that certain colors complement certain people. I loved my years of teaching and learning from patients, and helping them in any way I could. Over the years, I have been told I am good with color and that I could be an interior decorator. I considered that too, but I knew that becoming a DRES Stylist was the perfect blend of the things I love to do. I love to help people feel good about themselves. I love the creative part of putting outfits together—working with color, texture, and accessories. Organizing closets comes easy to me too, which many people find daunting.

I am here to dispute the old saying that "You can't teach an old dog new tricks." Even though I didn't realize it until recently, I have been reinventing myself—periodically learning new tricks—my whole life. I venture the same is true for you.

If your current reinvention has you unsure about what looks good on you or what colors give you that special glow, you deserve to treat yourself to a DRES Stylist consultation.

PAYING IT FORWARD

My sister and first client, Carolyn, shared her feelings about her difficulty with dressing herself and her DRES experience.

Carolyn's Story

"My experience with dressing myself has been a struggle to say the least. Most of my career I was lucky to wear uniforms so I did not have to dress myself. When I left my full-time position as a paramedic and started working in a professional office I struggled with matching clothes. When

Mary completed my colors and style consultation, I remember a sense of relief thinking I am going to finally be able to dress myself! We went shopping together and found a couple of clothing items that matched my colors and style. I was so excited!!! I came home and went shopping on my own feeling confident with my newfound knowledge!"

Many people, like my sister, ask me, "How often should you have a color analysis done?" As I learned, this isn't a "one and done" solution, as your coloring can change as you age. A good rule of thumb is to be reassessed every ten years, or any time you substantially change your hair color. The DRES System color analysis is much more customized than the old methods of color analysis, so your ultimate 42 colors really are your very best colors.

New Identity

I love being a DRES Stylist because I get to do some of the things I like best: organizing and streamlining closets, helping you learn to accessorize and put outfits together, giving you an honest opinion when we shop together, or function as a personal shopper if that is your desire. You will save lots of money by making your best clothing choices and buying only knockout pieces, thereby eliminating costly shopping mistakes.

Ultimately, you see that less clothing can mean more, because you will actually wear what you have, which helps you become more organized and efficient. You will have less stress because you won't have to dig through an overstuffed closet of things you don't wear. Most importantly, you will understand what styles look good on you and why. You probably know that a particular piece of clothing looks good on you, but you might not know why.

"Begin doing what you want to do now. We are not living in eternity. We have only this moment sparkling like a star in our hand and melting like a snowflake."

—Sir Francis Bacon

Be All You Can Be

More than anything, DRES Stylists are here to help you navigate through the maze of sales and marketing ploys out there trying to sell you the latest styles or fashions regardless if they flatter you or not. Having a DRES consultation is so much fun, and more than anything else, we want to help you shine and fully maximize your potential to "Be all you can be" (US Army motto). Helping you achieve your highest level of self-confidence is our goal.

The Four Steps to Reinventing Yourself

1) Accept that change is inevitable and necessary
2) Understand and formulate your personal identity
3) Take action to know yourself
4) Increase your self-confidence

Once you navigate these steps you will become your "authentic self" and you will experience happiness, contentment, fulfillment, and joy. I invite you to become your authentic self by seizing the day. Here's to you!

"Over the last year I lost a dramatic amount of weight and was faced with having to buy a whole new wardrobe. This was completely scary to me. Thanks to Mary's help, I now have an understanding of my 42 most complementary colors and the knowledge of how to dress my new body shape. I feel I can go shopping with confidence and ease. Now I am actually excited to go shopping!"

— Kaylynn Nelson (Sapphire)

Mary Angelosante
DRES System Certified Personal Stylist

Black Diamond, Washington
maryangelosante@gmail.com
dressystem.com

Mary Angelosante is an enthusiastic supporter of the DRES System and the ideals it stands for. Her goal is to help people define and express themselves in the manner they choose; thereby maximizing their self-image and their contribution to the people they touch. She enjoys blending her love for helping people with her love of clothing and jewelry, working as a DRES Personal Stylist.

As a military wife who moved seventeen times in twenty-six years, Mary became a master at moving as light and lean as possible. She also gained many organizational skills, like cleaning out closets, which she still utilizes today. In addition, she has displayed a flare and a great talent for decorating and color coordinating, which she used often while moving and setting up new homes. She has a tremendous appreciation for the lives military members and their families live, and the benefits, blessings, and sacrifices of military life.

Mary graduated with a BS in Nursing and worked intermittently while moving in the military. Most recently, she worked in an OB/GYN office for twelve years with women of all ages and stages of life. This experience provided her with the opportunity to help women with medical issues as well as life issues they shared with her. It was richly rewarding and she learned much from patients about life that she values and utilizes herself. She witnessed first-hand the strength, courage, fortitude, resilience, and beauty women possess. She would like to take this opportunity to thank all her patients for providing her with joy and a true richness of life!

Most important to Mary are the family and friends who have been a constant source of love and support over the years. She and her husband, Jim, have been married for thirty-four years and have two beautiful, successful daughters, Jennifer and Dawn. Mary enjoys hiking, gardening, decorating, and music as hobbies.

CHAPTER 5

SHINING THROUGH ADVERSITY

By Lori Goddard-Weed

I know the effects of adversity and I'm writing this chapter to provide a road map that may help guide you through your own challenges. When facing adversity, it is how you choose to react that defines you. I've made the choice to overcome and thrive for myself and for my children, which has required a lot of hard work, determination, and support from people who care deeply for me. Focus on loving yourself, surrounding yourself with supportive people, and finding a little joy each day. These are what will help you build your confidence and see yourself soar. It did for me.

I have a mantra that helps me: "My mess is my message in an authentic stylish way." In many ways, I feel as if I go about my days as a walking "hot mess." But, I am a *stylish* hot mess because dressing well, being stylish, and looking polished are the core of who I am. No matter what is going on in my life, I enjoy dressing well. It is what keeps me grounded. Being stylishly graceful is how I help women get through their own adversity. It's what I do. I guide women to look and feel their very best.

Maintaining a sense of confidence and always feeling your best can be achieved no matter what is going on in your life. Feeling unsure, sad, or overcome by grief is an opportunity for your confidence to wane. I call it my "hot messness." I've endured a lot of loss and I live with a high level of grief. You may be experiencing something similar. The feelings that go along with adversity are real and may always be present in your life. The key for me (and for you) is to make the choice to do something positive with our lives. Serving others is the best way to reduce the hold adversity may have on you.

There have been many times my confidence has lacked due to adversity, and I am thankful to be able to fall back on my faith, my sense of style, and the life tools

I have learned. I count my blessings every day. My many situations of adversity were not pleasant, but I knew that God, my family, and friends would help me get through my trials. When I look good, I feel good, which helps me build my confidence. I want to share with you the tools that help me.

In this chapter, I'm going to share my story and some information, tools, and healing exercises that I hope will guide you to 1) reclaim your confidence, 2) align your personal fashion styles, and 3) learn to take good care of yourself.

Even in the deepest, darkest days, I try to live by something I learned from author Regina Brett. "No matter how you feel, get up, dress up, and show up." By doing this, I felt better. I have never given up.

ADVERSITIES

My life's adversity is based around coping with grief. Over a period of sixteen years, I experienced an epic amount of loss. Matt, my husband of more than eleven years (and the father of my three sons), died of pancreatic cancer within five months of the diagnosis. Life threw a curveball at me; my dream of raising a family with Matt fell apart. Instead, I was a widow with two young boys, and six months pregnant with another. Coping on a day-to-day basis was difficult; there were days I wanted to give up.

I gained a lot of strength being a parent and watching my boys grow; supporting them as they learned to play various sports and accomplished milestones. My family and friends were a huge help to me as I learned to adjust to my new life alone. My faith was my foundation.

After five years of being on my own with my three boys, I was blessed to marry Kevin. Along with Kevin, I acquired a stepson, Matthew David, who was a treasured addition to the family. Life seemed to settle down. Of course, there were unexpected challenges. Kevin's employment changed and we had to get through two years of him being unemployed. During this time, our oldest son, Matthew David, returned home from his first military deployment to Afghanistan, and he struggled with the day-to-day life of civilian living stateside. But we all made it through.

For three years, our son Tony battled an addiction to prescription pain medication. As a family, we rallied together and supported him to go through an out-of-state drug rehabilitation program. After a three-month stay he came home as the vibrant, charming young man we all knew and loved. For a short time, life was smooth and I felt I could breathe again. But, at age twenty, Tony died of an accidental drug overdose. I was numb, in shock, and unsure how to handle it. The death of my child was a whole different loss than what I experienced when Matt died.

Finding Strength

Losing a child is difficult. Grieving the loss is a solitary journey that involves an ever-aching heart; the pain never goes away. I often wondered how I could continue living my life with such heartache.

Coping has been life changing. I realize no one can fix this, but with the grace of God I continue to get up and look my best each day. I'd like to share how I've overcome adversity, how I live with it every day, and how I hope to help others. Maybe I can even teach and show you how I have improved as a person, and how my life has become fabulous even in the midst of loss.

I could go on and on about my back story but what I'd really like to do is share what I've learned. I have discovered that my commitment to looking well, no matter what life throws at me, is my foundation for helping others with their personal fashion style. This, in turn, has helped my healing.

When I was first widowed, I belonged to two wonderful support groups, one for young widows and one for young moms. Each group met once a week; both were my saving grace. The women encouraged me to express my true feelings; they listened and supported me. If you find you are struggling, asking for help may be the beginning of taking care of yourself and building relationships that may last a lifetime.

"Our prayers are answered not when we are given what we ask, but when we are challenged to be what we can."

—Morris Adler

Finding Inspiration

In this chapter, I share about the biggest losses of that sixteen-year period of time in my life. However, there were more. My father died suddenly and unexpectedly. A close and dear friend lost a battle with cancer. Our other two boys struggled with their own daily grief, the family lost two pets within months of each other, and my mother was diagnosed with incurable breast cancer. I'm impressed with how she has handled the adversity in her life—losing her husband and now fighting the effect of chemotherapy. She's my role model.

We thought the adversity was behind us, but then my second husband Kevin was in an accident while on a nine-day climbing trip in the Cascade Mountains with five of his friends. He fell 1,200 feet and had to be air lifted to the hospital for treatment. He had a lot of physical injuries and a serious head injury.

Today, he is doing well, but he still has challenges with pain from the accident. Kevin, a true athlete and participant in Ironman triathlons, was told he could never swim again due to the injuries to his arm. This news was devastating because swimming is one of his passions. His determination and commitment to healing are inspiring; beyond being a man who should not have survived a tremendous fall, he amazes me daily. One year after his accident (and looking very fashionable in his wetsuit I might add) Kevin participated in a half Ironman competition and placed in the top of his age bracket.

Having to deal with both Tony's passing and Kevin's near-death experience, I wasn't sure how I felt; I was in survivor mode. Again, my faith and my commitment to dressing well were my foundation. Daily, I told myself, "I can do this" as I supported Kevin. During these most difficult times, I made sure to notice how garments were working or not working for Kevin. He lost the use of his arm temporarily, which made it difficult for him to get dressed.

Finding Comfort

My life is full of adversity—and it wasn't how I wanted life to go. I was a mess and sometimes I still am, but I have learned that it is okay to be a mess at times. The emotions never go away and grief has a mind of its own; sometimes it takes control and affects me in a way that I'm not sure how to handle. I get anxious and emotional. I worry for no reason and often question how I will get through my grief.

I take deep breaths, lean on my faith, family, and friends for support and try to use my skills of making lists, setting goals, and planning out the days of my week to cope. In the end, I always have to dig deep inside where my faith resides and the spark of life flickers—where it is still present inside me—to survive. Being stylish and graceful is my comfort, knowing that I look and feel my best for that given day.

"Even in the face of adversity, fashion remains an important pursuit."

—Diane Von Furstenberg

RECLAIMING YOUR CONFIDENCE

When facing life's obstacles, it's easy to lose your confidence. But do not worry because confidence can be restored by looking good and feeling fabulous. That's why I help women focus on fashion, their personal style, and embracing their inner beauty. Feeling good about yourself and what your life is about is key to reclaiming your sense of confidence.

Ever since I was a young girl, I have enjoyed fashion. I love seeing how people pull together different outfits. I learned to love fashion from my mother who was a huge influence in my life. Her wardrobe was incredible with so many beautiful, one-of-a-kind articles of clothing she bought at boutiques. When my mom walked out the front door she looked like a million bucks with her matching handbags and shoes, her hair and makeup nicely done. Mom taught me to embrace my inner beauty while expressing it on the outside, which is what I hope to inspire you to do as well. Being authentic to your fashion style will lead to your improved sense of confidence.

Your appearance represents both your personal and fashion styles. Some people are innovators while others follow classic, traditional trends. Whatever your choice, feeling good and believing in yourself are what matter most when it comes to presenting your best self to the world.

Here are some questions to consider to discover what makes you feel the best about yourself:

What is your passion in life? Make a list of your passions and explore why they are important to you.

Is your fashion style matching your personal style in a way you want to be portrayed? List your fashion styles and activities.

Are your garments the right color and fit for you and do you feel beautiful wearing them? What are some of your favorites?

What are the fears/obstacles that make you lack confidence?

What is your image of your best self?

When you lack confidence, where does it originate? Do you know?

How would you describe your belief in yourself?

Are you accepting the guidance and support being offered to you?

What inspires you to get up every day?

GUIDANCE TO BUILD YOUR CONFIDENCE

Your life is a journey of peaks and valleys. There will be times that your confidence will soar and times it may feel flatlined. Here are a few things I've found useful to restore my confidence in those times when it wanes. You, too, might find them useful.

- Know your faith or spiritual being, the core of who you are
- Have respect for yourself, others, and your surroundings
- Be authentic and embrace the beautiful you
- Write out goal cards and visualize your goals
- Hang with positive/like-minded people to generate positive energy

- Know your values
- Face your struggles with poise and grace
- Be kind to yourself and know that you are awesome
- Take baby steps; change doesn't occur overnight
- Live, love, and especially laugh

"I have always believed that fashion was not only to make women more beautiful, but also to reassure them, give them more confidence."

—Yves Saint Laurent

Watching my clients' confidence grow is a gratifying feeling for me, achieving even the smallest goal is always a wonderful accomplishment. I feel that my clients' personal styles and fashion styles are about finding that inner strength that we all may lack at times. I help guide my clients in finding the right color, fit, and style that showcases their body's best attributes. Once you master the right balance, your inner beauty will shine with poise and grace. Your overall image combined with your style is based on the desires you want to portray. Set your standards at a level that works within your goals, because you are a beautiful woman. When you look and feel good, you shine bright from the inside out. By embracing life to the fullest you can learn to build your confidence.

Here is what a couple of clients have to say...

"Lori, thank you so much, for your DRES consulting services! I have gone from dreading to shop to loving it! Now that I know the styles and colors that are right for me, it gives me confidence. I am not overwhelmed anymore when I walk into a store. I know what to look for and how to add pieces to what I already have to create more wardrobe options. Now when I look in my closet, I know that I will look great in anything I pick out. I love my color palette. It is such a handy tool and I have had many ask how they can get one. I am definitely sending them your way."

—Chris (Emerald)

"Lori, thank you so much for our session. I learned so much in just the two hours we spent together. For the first time in a long time, I can actually say that I am looking forward to shopping, now that I know which styles and colors will work for me. The DRES System made so much sense to me and also helped me understand why all those clothes I got "on sale" just sit in my closet—not so much a bargain after all. Being a school teacher, I cannot imagine swaying from the sale racks too much but your assistance will definitely help narrow my search and make me feel more comfortable and confident in the clothes I wear."

—Kathy (Sapphire)

KEEPING YOUR PERSONAL AND FASHION STYLES ALIGNED

Dressing to fit your personal and fashion styles is important because it gives you the confidence to believe in yourself and enjoy who you are. I help guide my clients to make sure these two coexist. Personal style is learning about who you are, how you would like to be portrayed, and being your best and authentic self. It exemplifies your personality and is your first communication as you walk into a room.

WHAT IS YOUR PERSONAL STYLE?

Earlier in the book, you read about the DRES System personal styles (Classic, Chic, Romantic, Ethnic, Dramatic). As you think about your personality and how you want to come across in the world, which of the styles best describes you?

Being able to describe your inner beauty and strengths will help you in defining your personal style, especially the characteristics you love about yourself. What words best describe you? Are you compassionate, kind-hearted, caring, gentle, direct, or distant? How about thoughtful, cautious, approachable, straight forward, or disciplined?

List all the best words you would use to describe yourself.

If you're having difficulties making a list, ask a close friend what they like about you. How do they perceive the inner beauty that shines so brilliantly from within you?

DISCOVERING YOUR SIGNATURE STYLE

Once you have determined your personal style you can move on to determining your own signature style, which is an outfit or item that you wear and is unique to you. It can be as simple as a handbag, a beautiful scarf, or a broach that you always wear, which reminds people of you when they see it. Here are some examples of people you may recognize. Ellen DeGeneres likes to wear button-down shirts and a vest to match. Lady Gaga's extravagant costumes have become her trademark. When Barbara Bush was First Lady, we became accustomed to seeing her beautiful strand of pearls.

Living in the Pacific Northwest I tend to always have a cardigan on or tied around my shoulders in case there is a chill in the air. During the cooler months, I add a scarf that coordinates with the cardigan.

"Elegance is not standing out, but being remembered."

—Giorgio Armani

WHAT PERSONAL STYLE COMMUNICATES

When a woman lacks personal style, this communicates that she also lacks confidence in who she is or wants to become. Remember, first impressions are very important so make sure your personal style is speaking correctly.

There are two types of communication: verbal (what you say) and nonverbal (what you do and wear). Your visual presence often speaks much louder than what you say. Even though your words make a smaller impression, make sure the volume, tone, and pitch of your voice are professional.

Posture conveys 38 percent of your nonverbal image. Albert Mehrabian, a professor of psychology and thought leader towards this statistic, is best known for his publication on the relative importance of verbal and nonverbal messaging (https://en.wikipedia.org/wiki/Albert_Mehrabian). Standing tall conveys confidence. You only have a few seconds to make that first impression and if you look like you've got it together you will exude confidence and will attract people to you. You will be highly approachable, which builds trust and likability.

"Style is a way to say who you are without having to speak."

—Rachel Zoe

DISCOVERING YOUR FASHION STYLE

Answering some simple questions can help you to begin developing your fashion style. Establishing your signature style requires self-awareness, confidence, personality, and creativeness. Style equals your individuality, and a signature style is that unique touch for which you are known and recognized. I hope the following questions will help you get to know yourself better:

When it comes to fashion, what do you struggle with the most (accessorizing, selecting colors, outfit styling, shopping, something else)?

What are your fashion likes?

What are your fashion dislikes?

What colors make you feel good when you wear them?

What looks and feels great on your body shape?

I have learned it is okay to feel as if I'm a hot mess and at the same time appear all put together. Being your best each and every day is all anyone can ask of you. Being authentic to who you are in your personal and fashion style is what is most important.

Next, look through magazines to discover the styles, colors, and specific clothes to which you're most attracted. This is a very fun exercise and will reveal a lot about your fashion style.

Then, let a stylist help you determine your body shape and perform a color analysis. The insights you'll gain from this process will teach you how to highlight your beautiful body assets and accentuate the colors that make you glow. As you educate yourself on how to put the proper garments and colors together you will see the fashion diva come out and your confidence will increase.

LOVE YOUR STYLE: BOTH PERSONAL AND FASHION

Developing your personal and fashion style takes time and is a journey that everyone can enjoy. Choosing a fashion style is all about who you are and what your life is about. You want to make sure you are choosing a fashion style that fits your personality because clothing is a reflection of your self-image and how you portray it. Remember this: combining how you want to be perceived by others with your own personal desires leads to the alignment of your personal and fashion styles.

An individual style reflects your personal style and builds confidence as you become more in tune with who you are as a unique individual. Here are some questions to consider:

- What type of job do you have or desire?
- What is the dress code for your desired profession?
- How do you spend most of your time during the week and weekend?
- How well does your closet reflect your personal and professional priorities?
- Do you wear an item because it feels right and allows your inner beauty to shine brightly?

Understanding both your personal and fashion style allows you to become more confident in shopping for your unique body shape, fit, and your best colors. As these two styles coexist, you may alleviate the stress that you once felt entering a store. Your ideal wardrobe takes time to build. Once you understand your personal and fashion style needs you will become confident in building a wardrobe of quality, not quantity.

My client Sandy had a lot of anxiety shopping in stores and had no confidence in her decision making. She felt she struggled with what looked good on her and what to buy. As we worked together, she began to embrace her beautiful body shape and defined illusion, and she learned how to show her best attributes. Now, she understands her best colors, what angles and garment cuts works best for her, and she has fully embraced her beauty. She is confident in every piece she wears.

When you walk into a room looking sharp, polished, and ready to engage with others, they will respond to you positively. We all have challenges; getting dressed may be one you struggle with each morning. Take it in stride and prepare for your day the night before. Being organized will help build your confidence. When you understand your desired image and style, your obstacles become less of a challenge.

YOUR CLOSET TELLS A STORY

Your closet is a very personal room in your life. Within its doors are the history of your life and the story of the authentic, real, and unique you. As you assess and start to intentionally choose clothes, colors, and accessories that align with your personal and fashion styles, your story will emerge.

I live with a lot of grief, but my grief doesn't define me and isn't reflected in my closet, which is full of color, and shows me fully. Through adversity, your fashion style and your personal style are an outward representation of who you are authentically. I don't have to get dressed wearing a billboard sign telling everyone I'm a widow with three small children, or I'm a mother who lost her son due to a drug overdose. I get to dress up as Lori, who I am authentically, regardless of the adversity that is challenging me daily. My closet is full of color because color makes me feel alive.

As we assess the contents of your closet, you may discover that you're holding onto items that no longer serve you, but for some reason you can't let them go. It's because each item of clothing has its own story, oftentimes representing dear memories. Some examples may be your wedding dress, or a t-shirt you received after finishing your first 5k event.

Chris' Story

A wonderful client of mine has some Pendleton wool skirts that she really loves, but wondered if they were outdated. Together we tried different lengths of hem lines and found the perfect one for Chris' height. The skirts are classic, and ideal for her professional wardrobe. The color and fit are now perfect for her gem shape. All they needed was to be shortened. With the simple change of a new hemline for these skirts, we were able to create several new outfits. Tweaking your items a little may be all you need for a quick update. Make sure you have a reliable seamstress to work with if you are altering your favorite items.

Your closet expresses who you are. Sometimes we need to let go of the past in order to make room for something brand new. There are items I think you should hang onto, while others should find new homes. Hang on to items that add positive value to your personal and fashion styles; they are in good-to-excellent condition and are being well taken care of. Let go of items cluttering up your personal and fashion style.

Consider these questions as you sort through the items in your closet to determine if they are keepers or if they need to find a new home:

- Does the item build your confidence?
- Does your item currently fit your gem shape properly?
- Do you feel vibrant in the color?
- Do you really need the item you are hanging onto?
- When was the last time you wore the piece in question?

If you don't know the answer to this last question, use the backward hanger trick. Turn all hangers in your closet facing backwards and as you wear an item turn the hanger the proper way when you put it back. After the season has passed, check to see what items you have worn or not worn. If you didn't wear something, maybe it is time to find the backwards hanger item a new home.

Jan's Story

My client, Jan, became a widow at the young age of twenty-six. She has a dress that she keeps tucked in her closet that she wore at her husband's funeral. She understands that she will never wear it again, nor wants to, but she feels the need to hang on to it. Jan, now in her fifties, has been married for several years, raised two beautiful children and is passionate about life. Even though her dress continues to hang in the back of her closet, she understands the importance of knowing that her story is unique to her and how her personal and fashion styles coexist. Jan looks and feels confident in her wardrobe and dresses beautifully.

What do the clothes in your closet have to say about you and your life? I am here to help you live authentically and make wardrobe choices that align with your personal and fashion styles. As a result, the grasp your adversities have on you will lessen over time. And, as your confidence continues to climb, you will become more in control and understand who you are. Live your best life knowing who you are.

TAKING CARE OF YOURSELF

People perceive you as confident when you are dressed well and when you take care of yourself physically. Doing so will also improve your overall mental stamina and your sense of well-being. Taking care of yourself and staying healthy are important, so I have listed some exercises for you to try.

Healing exercises can be good for the soul. Find what may work for you and use it. As time goes on, you may need to use a different practice, or go back to one that you have already used. As for myself, these five practices have helped me on a daily basis. I have become a stronger woman and moved forward by taking baby steps.

CREATE A SAFE ENVIRONMENT

Creating an environment where you feel safe and can share anything without being judged is vitally important. Find a counselor, friend, or a support group that you trust. My support groups were what helped me after Matt died. I needed to be with people who were experiencing similar feelings. It also helped to be with friends who just let me talk as they listened with no judgment.

Seeking help from a friend, counselor, or a mentor may be what you need to move forward.

ESTABLISH A PRACTICE OF CONTEMPLATION

My faith, the little spark that flickers way down deep inside me, has helped guide me in overcoming my own adversities. On those days when I didn't think I would make it to the next hour, reading an inspiring quote or scripture always provided me a boost.

I especially like Psalms 18:32: "He fills me with strength and protects me whenever I go." And Philippians 4:13: "I can do all things through Christ who strengthens me."

If sitting, meditating, getting lost in soft music, or going to a yoga class helps you, then do it. Allow yourself time to heal and be kind to yourself. As time passes, the type of quietness you desire may change and your inner confidence builds.

WRITE AND USE AFFIRMATIONS

Life is short no matter how good or bad your day is going. I know this personally from experience. Negative thinking is not healthy and will lead to sabotaging your own belief in yourself and those around you. Maintaining a positive attitude leads to being a happier, healthier person than those whose attitude and thinking is negative.

Here are a few examples of positive affirmations:

- I look and feel confidently beautiful in everything I own in my closet
- I easily and effortlessly walk around my obstacles
- I feel vibrant, lively, and am filled with energy

TRY THIS MIRROR EXERCISE:

Stand in front of mirror and look at yourself. Look into your own eyes. Say this affirmation:

______ (your name), I love you. You are beautiful and confident. You are a perfect gem just the way you are. You are unique and brilliant.

VISUALIZE THE LIFE YOU DESIRE

What are your short- and long-term goals? Give some thought to these questions:

What do you want to have happen in the next week?

What do you want to have happen in the next month?

What do you want to have happen in the next year?

What do you want to have happen in the next five years?

From my personal experience, answering these questions was very difficult in the midst of my grieving. If you, too, are feeling this way during your adversity ask yourself this question: What do you want to have happen *today*? I was in a state of mind that looking past the hours in my day was too exhausting. I had days that my only goal was to wash the dishes and if I accomplished that one task, it was a great day.

SETTING GOALS

Having goals and then taking the necessary steps to achieve them is important as you look to overcome any kind of adversity. We all need things to look forward to. Setting goals is a step toward making good things happen.

Allow yourself time to work through your adversity. You are in charge and you can set the pace. Just be aware if you start to feel stuck, remember to ask for help.

Visualizing who you are and the changes you want to make, personally and professionally, is powerful and it works. As you visualize your life, give form to what you desire by thinking it, saying it, and writing it. Your confidence will definitely escalate and you will achieve what you desire.

One of my goals was to exercise a little more. I was challenged by a friend to walk 100 miles a month, to which I laughed and asked if the miles flying from Washington to Arizona counted. There was no way I thought I could walk that much in thirty days. But, as I thought about it I realized that all I'd have to do is walk about 3.5 miles a day. That seemed doable. In fact, I was an over achiever; I walked over 100 miles before the month ended and I felt great. Getting out of my comfort zone and spending active time with myself and with friends has become routine for me. My mind is clearer, I have a lot of energy, and my clothes fit well.

On weekends, my husband Kevin will go for a run one way and meet back up with me for his cool down. We walk together on the trail, ending at a local coffee shop for a treat. Exercising and sharing time with him is one of the highlights of my week.

Making Lists

Making a "to do" list is similar to setting goals. When I feel overwhelmed by the number of tasks I have to accomplish, making a list is one of the ways I alleviate my anxiety. I like to get things done and I love the sense of accomplishment I feel as I take a pen and cross a task off my list.

> *"Make lists of your strengths and be aware of what you are good at, believe in yourself and your abilities."*
>
> —Maria Shriver

Write in a Journal

I'm not great at journaling, but I do try. Here is an exercise I did that helped me a lot. I hope you find it helpful, too. There's no right way to do it; you can bullet list items like I have in the example, or elaborate with a lot of detail. Journaling is personal and is only for you.

I found this exercise to be helpful and very healing, but it was also emotional. It helped me process and understand feelings from day one. The important part of the exercise was connecting how my adversity has helped me become the person I am today.

What Happened?	Initial Emotion	What Helped Me Cope?	How Have I Transformed?
Son died	Disbelief, devastated, shocked	Faith, family, and friends	I am a fighter and I've made the choice to continue on

"Grief never ends...But it changes. It's a passage, not a place to stay. Grief is not a sign of weakness, nor a lack of faith...it is the price of LOVE."

—Author Unknown

Adversity touches us all in some way. How you approach it and deal with it is up to you. Are you respecting yourself and trying your best at this moment? Are you aware of your desired image and what you would like to portray to the world? Are you authentic to who you are and want to be?

I believe in you and I know that you have the courage inside of you to shine brilliantly through your adversity. Our obstacles may never truly go away, but they soften over time. Here are a few tips to remember along the journey:

- It's okay to laugh and enjoy yourself during difficult times. Laughter is definitely the best policy
- Show the grace and emotions of your story. Faith, family, and friends will get you through life's difficult circumstances
- Embrace change
- Inspire people and learn from one another
- Everyone has a different story that is unique; embrace yours fully

"You can have anything you want in life if you dress for it."

—Edith Head

Get up, dress up, and live up to what you want in your life every day. Reclaim your confidence. Make sure your personal style and fashion style are aligned and take care of yourself. Being successful in these daily priorities will add brightness to your life and ease the obstacles you face daily. Everyone is a mess at times; our hot messness is our message. It's quirky, unique, and authentic to each of us.

Your journey is a special story that is told best from your own passionate heart. Finding what fulfills you spiritually will help guide you to an awesome, confident, and fabulous you. May your confidence in your personal and fashion style shine bright, just as you do.

Thank you for letting me share the message of my story. Remember, shining brightly through our adversity is a journey, not a destination.

"I cannot say enough about my DRES Stylist Lori. She is kind, considerate, classy, timeless, and fun. She came into my world and made stepping out of my closet a whole new experience! Seriously she helped me step outside of my box and encouraged me to use what I had by mixing things up and yet staying with basics. Only a highly trained eye can do this and Lori is highly trained! I embrace my gem shape and feel confident in all that I wear now. I recommend Lori to anyone who is looking to enhance their own confidence in building the right wardrobe for themselves. Thanks Lori, you're a true gem."

— Jan (Emerald)

Lori Goddard-Weed
DRES System Certified Personal Stylist
and Director of Events

Snohomish, Washington
imageisit@gmail.com
dressystem.com

Lori Goddard-Weed is an author and speaker on personal image, style, and building confidence through adversity. She is a Certified Personal Stylist, a certified etiquette instructor with the acclaimed Final Touch Finishing School and is also the Director of Events for DRES. Through workshops and seminars, Lori provides knowledge to enhance women's understanding of fashion, fit, and their overall image.

Lori earned her Bachelor of Science degree from Oregon State University. Her emphasis was Fashion Merchandise and Business Administration. While attending OSU, Lori was active in Panhellenic Recruitment Council, her sorority, Alpha Gamma Delta, and was 1st runner-up for Miss OSU. She also coordinated the spring fashion show for Mom's Weekend. Lori has worked in the fashion industry for over 30 years. With sixteen years of experience in retail management, Lori also models (in print and on the runway) and has been featured in television commercials.

Lori's passion for fashion and image is a wonderful combination for helping her client's improve their overall appearance and confidence both personally and professionally. They feel comfortable exploring their unique body shape and enhancing their beautiful assets. Lori teaches that personal style is about finding inner confidence, understanding lifestyle, and being authentic.

Lori is active civically as a volunteer in many arenas, including Providence General Children's Association, The YMCA's Bright Future of America's Children, Queen It's a New Day, and the public school system in her hometown. Professionally, she is a member of a national group called the Femfessional Group for Women. Lori enjoys walking, skiing, and gardening and she resides in Snohomish, Washington, with her husband, three boys, and fluffy kitties.

"Your best fashion style is how you overcome adversity."

—Lori Goddard-Weed

CHAPTER 6

THE CLOSET CLEANSE

By Wendy Petersen

Do you sometimes feel that you are the only woman on the planet who struggles with keeping her closet organized and deciding what to wear each day?

Do you stare at your closet with nothing to wear every morning?

Do you hate to shop?

When you do shop, do you end up buying the same things over and over again?

Do you feel in a rut when it comes time to put an outfit together?

365 Days

This chapter is meant to put an end to your struggle. Using the suggestions here, I invite you to devote the next 365 days to:

1) Cleaning out your closet
2) Curating a closet that's full of wardrobe pieces you love wearing
3) Up-leveling the way you dress yourself. As a result, your confidence will soar as you dress with ease and receive compliments about your appearance

During the course of the year, I hope you'll view me as your very own "fashion whisperer," the supportive voice in your ear helping you to follow the guidelines in this chapter. I promise that your closet will be refreshed and organized, you will have a stress-free (10-minute) system for getting dressed each morning, and your confidence in choosing outfits will skyrocket.

The reason I have chosen 365 days to go through this process of up-leveling your wardrobe is because it takes time to curate a wardrobe you love. Ideally, everything in your closet will be items that make you feel your best, and look great on you. On TV, it happens in half an hour with $5,000. In real life, it takes time, budgeting, some guidelines, and clarity about expectations.

It's really important to be clear about where you want to go in regards to your wardrobe. To help you, I have posed some questions for you to consider. If fashion is not your "genius zone," then you're reading the right book. Refer back to your answers over the next year to keep yourself centered on your goals of dressing to be your most authentic self.

How do you want to dress? How do you want to show up in the world?

How do you want others to see you? What colors are you wearing? Be descriptive.

What/Who do you want to look like? What is your vision for your best version of you?

Describe someone in your workplace that always looks pulled together. What do you like about their outfit? What would you change?

How do you want others to perceive you? Is it important that you dress and feel trustworthy? Sexy? Responsible? Smart? To dress this way, what would you wear?

Are you ready to start buying clothes in a new way? Are you ready to start inviting something new into your life?

Building closet and wardrobe confidence is something many people have to work on. Most of us don't have a big chunk of money for a one-time shopping trip to make a lot of new purchases. That's why I propose our year-long journey together. Plus, as the seasons of the year change, so do fabrics, colors, and the style of the clothes. Building your closet up over four quarters is the best way to take on this exciting endeavor I call closet cleansing. When you look back a year from now you will be amazed at the progress you've made.

CLEANING OUT YOUR CLOSET

Closet Cleansing Process

A true wardrobe cleanout gets rid of many pieces at once, analyzing every piece. It includes organizing by creating three piles: donation, sentimental, and alteration. Cleaning out your closet is a great way to invite something new into your life. If done correctly, the process of going through this should take only a few hours. Closet cleansing is not a one-off donation process. It is a complete overhaul. Let's get started.

What's the Approach for You?

There are three ways to approach the closet cleanse: do it by yourself, get help from a friend, or hire a professional.

1) Doing It Alone

Cleaning out your closet by yourself can leave you feeling overwhelmed and sometimes with an unfinished project on your hands. Often times it does not have the desired outcome that hiring someone to help you would have. It's easy to get distracted at your house, especially when the phone rings, or the laundry buzzer goes off. It's also easy to keep more things than you give away because, "well, one day I might..." or "this was given to me by..." or "when I lose 10 pounds..." and then you end up keeping many of the pieces that are taking up the most space, which you never wear anyway. If you do choose to tackle this project by yourself, be critical. If clothing does not fit, donate. If you haven't worn it in eight months, donate.

2) Getting Help from a Friend

Asking a friend to help you can be fun. Get someone who will give you an honest opinion and keep you on track. I find that blocking out one hour at a time to tackle everything works well with a friend in tow. Set a timer and conquer the hardest section first.

3) Hiring a Professional

Inviting a professional to help you clean out your closet—someone you don't know—can be a scary proposition. But, potentially, it is the best way to organize and get the job done. Because we clean out closets for a living, we're efficient, well organized, and very complete. When I work with my clients, I always ask them to visualize what they want in their life. I want them to tell me or write down what they are trying to attract. This could be anything from a new car to a new relationship. Regardless of what you want, you must make room for the new thing. By hiring a professional, you are taking steps to create space for what you desire. Your closet is a great place to start creating more space.

Many people say they are embarrassed to invite me into their closet. They say things like, "I wouldn't want anyone to see my mess." Rest assured, a professional doesn't care about your mess. As a stylist, I have seen it all. Dust bunnies, hidden items, cat hair, and a lot of unmentionables are the norm. And, as for the mess, do not clean up before we arrive to do the work. That's why you hire us.

You will feel so refreshed once the cleaning has occurred. It feels good to let go, and there is something magical about having a clean space. A huge benefit is feeling a sense of completion, satisfaction, and openness to a clean closet. Asking/hiring someone to help you clean out your closet will be one of the best decisions you'll ever make.

LET'S GET STARTED

STEP 1: Visualization
Visualize what you are welcoming into your life. The 'new' car/relationship/ whatever you want. In order for that new 'thing' to come into your life, you have to know what you want. Be specific, dream big, and be honest. A great place to start making more room for your vision is in your closet.

STEP 2: Standardize Your Hangers
I recommend buying the thin, velvet, black hangers. They are skinny and will create so much more space in your closet. Secondly, the velvet helps to grip your clothes, so that one shoulder won't fall off the hanger (think of that annoying camisole that won't stay put). These velvet hangers work like a charm. Having all the same hanger in your closet is magical and aesthetically pleasing. It's calming to the eye and makes a world of difference. I don't recommend the white plastic hangers. They take up more room than necessary and do not grip clothes well. Give wire hangers back to the dry cleaner.

STEP 3: Empty Your Closet
Before you start cleaning out your closet, it's really important to gather every single piece of clothing you own. This means the coats in the coat closet, stashed dresses in the guest bedroom, and the few pairs of pants that are hanging in your husband's closet. Bring everything—*every last piece of clothing you own.* Now you are ready to start making decisions about what to keep and what to toss. It is easy to get overwhelmed at this point and want to give up, but trust me. This process is fun with a friend or a professional and it is a sure-fire way to make room for something new in your life.

STEP 4: Decision-Making Time

As you go through every item in your closet, the most important question that I use with all of my clients is to ask, "Does this item make me feel like a 10?" If it doesn't make you feel like a 10, get rid of it. I'm also talking about your pajamas. Replace it with something that does. Be harsh and decisive. Remember, we are up-leveling your confidence and your clothes, and it's really important to make a distinction between something that is a beautiful piece of clothing versus something that makes you *feel beautiful*. The latter is preferred.

Questions to Consider

- Is this item in good condition? Does it have paint stains, holes, and pilling?
- Is the item up-to-date? If you purchased it ten years ago, probably not. A decade is a long time to hold onto a piece of clothing. Just like everything in your refrigerator has an expiration date on it, so does everything in your closet. Let's clean it out, girl!
- Is it the right color for you? Is the item missing a button, or does it need an alteration?
- Does it make you feel like a 10? Does it bring you joy?
- Does it fit you today (not when you lose 15 pounds)?

You Love the Shirt, but Never Wear It

Here's a scenario I experience often with my clients:

> **Client:** *"I love this shirt. The color, the fabric...it's beautiful. Just look at this design! Isn't it gorgeous? The problem is every time I put it on, it doesn't fit me right. So I always end up taking it off and never wearing it."*

Do you have a piece of clothing in your closet like this? What do you do with it in this case?

> **Wendy:** *You thank the blouse for coming into your life and give it away. Give thanks that the item showed you what you love in fashion and go shopping to replace it. The blouse taught you everything you need to know about finding another beautiful piece of clothing.*

A Sentimental Item

You might ask, "What if the item has sentimental value to me?" Great! Let's keep it, but *not* hanging in your closet. I worked with a client who had the dress she wore on her very first date with her husband. They've been married twenty-six years. Clearly, this dress holds value for her, and she should keep it. Although she is never going to wear it again, it needs to be put in a safe place. This is a great opportunity to create a special bin or box that holds your treasures and fond memories. The goal is to have everything in your closet be something you can wear and makes you feel like a 10. That way, you can go and get dressed in the morning with complete confidence, knowing that your closet is home to working articles of clothing that make you feel good.

STEP 5: Putting Your Closet Back Together

Organize by Color

Once you have purged everything and made decisions about what to keep and what to toss or alter, organize your closet by color. This is the most efficient way to find any piece of clothing. Whenever you can't seem to find that black blouse, you won't have to rifle through a disheveled closet. You will automatically know that it is hanging in the black section. No time will be squandered looking for an item that is hidden between two other blouses.

Organize by Event

For some of my working-mom clients, I find organizing their closet by event is better suited for them. I have heard over and over again that when they shop, they try to "double-dip." They will buy a piece of clothing to wear to their son's soccer games and to work, too. Since I'm in the habit of trying to help people dress well, and dress *better*, I help them make decisions about what to wear to work, and what to wear on weekends. They should be different pieces. Yes, it's okay to buy a beautiful blouse just *for work*. It's okay to purchase something nice and cute for yourself only for the weekends. So we organize by event. Part of their closet represents "wear-to-work" clothes. A section may represent "weekend or casual-wear," a "workout" section, and a section dedicated to clothes for supporting their local professional sports team. Organizing by event lets them know exactly what section of the closet to go to when getting dressed.

Only Keep and Buy What You Love
Buy clothing that makes you feel amazing, even pajamas. They don't necessarily have to be amazing and sexy pajamas. They can simply be comfortable cat print pajamas that help you get a good night's sleep.

80-20 RULE

Often, I see closets full of clothes, but hardly any of them are worn. People usually wear about 20 percent of their closet, 80 percent of the time. This means the other pieces of clothing hanging in there are collecting dust. They aren't being worn, and are only taking up space. My advice is to purge those pieces and create space for the 10s in your life. Less is more when it comes to closets and fashion.

THE ISSUES YOU MAY ENCOUNTER

As you are going through the closet cleansing process, you may encounter some resistance. Things like, "Well, I might wear this..." or "What if I need it...." or "I need to lose 10 more pounds, then it will fit." Read on for guidance on how to address these issues as they arise. Note: this is where hiring a professional comes in handy. Professionals stop the buck when the resistance creeps up.

Too Big vs. Too Small
While you are cleaning out your closet, try on the clothes. If an item doesn't fit you, get rid of it. If the item is too small, do not hold onto it hoping to lose the weight. It's really important to keep clothes that fit you well and bring you the most joy when you wear them. You must start dressing for the size and shape of your body, *today*. Do not wait to dress your best until you are a certain weight and do not hold onto clothes that are too small for your shape with the hopes of one day fitting into them again. I call those clothes, "I'm too fat for that" clothes.

Every day, when you go to get dressed, you open your closet and the "I'm too fat for that" clothes are waiting there sticking their tongue out at you. The best thing you can do for yourself in this case is replace them with clothes that love your body for the shape and size it is today.

The same goes for clothes that are too big. I have many clients who have shed many pounds, but their fear is that one day they may need those large-sized clothes again. Let them go. Free yourself from the trap of "what if." Do not hold onto the past, or your fear. By releasing these items, you will create so much space for something new in your life. Let go of the fear.

Waiting to Lose Weight

One point I really want to drive home is about confidence vs. weight loss. I hear from women all the time they are "waiting to lose weight" before going shopping. More often than not, from the looks of what they are wearing, it looks to me like they have been waiting a long time. I don't say that to be harsh. Rather, I say it as a reality check. Waiting to lose weight is a nasty trap that many of us fall into. I want to make the argument that by dressing your body for the size and shape it is today, right now, you will walk straighter and you will appear slimmer and more confident. You will command a different presence and you may even want to start a nutrition program because you are finally treating yourself the way you should be treated. You are dressing yourself with respect.

Finally, ban the mentality of, "I'm getting ready-to-get-ready-to-get-ready before I present myself to the world." Present yourself every day to the world as if you care about who you are. Show your children, your partner, and your co-workers the respect you have for yourself, and soon you will notice others treating you differently. Whether you are a stay-at-home parent or the CEO of a bank, it's time to stop using weight as an excuse not to look good and dress well.

I have had many clients who, after working with me, start a nutrition program and lose weight. They lost so much weight that the clothes we purchased together didn't fit. They said it was the best money they ever spent. Spending money to buy all those clothes to finally start dressing their larger frames with respect paid off. The weight loss was an afterthought. They didn't buy the clothes with the intent to lose weight. They bought the clothes with the intent to up-level their look, show up in the world, and feel good about themselves. All this time, they were afraid to spend money on new clothes because of their weight, but the weight loss followed with their shift in perception about themselves.

Forgotten Items in Your Closet

Have you ever said, "I forgot I had this. This is a cute pair of pants! I'm keeping them." The reality is, if you haven't worn them since last year, are you really going to wear them again? How long have they been sitting in your closet/drawer, forgotten? It may be time to let them go. Don't talk yourself into keeping things that you forgot you had.

CURATING A WARDROBE YOU LOVE

This is where you get to fill in the blanks after cleaning everything out. It feels so good to get rid of things, and it feels equally as good to purchase something new that fits you well. Below is a guide to help you shop to find the perfect items to fill your new space with lovely 10s. Remember, restocking your wardrobe takes place over time, as the seasons change. It rarely happens in one shopping trip, so keep the long-term goal, the 365 days, in the back of your mind as you shop.

The way in which you show up in the world and how you project yourself is very much in tune with how others will treat you. So think about how you want to be treated at work, at home, at school, and at the bar. When you have that image in your head of who you want to be, take a look at your newly cleaned-out closet. Does it reflect who you want to be? If it's not there yet, let's use the next 365 days to get there!

Buying Sale Items

Many people assume that it costs a lot of money to look really pulled together. Though it does not cost *a lot* of money to look and feel really pulled together, it does cost *some* money. Expect to spend some money in this area of your life. It will be worth every penny, if done strategically. Do not buy something just because it's on sale. The "sale syndrome" used to affect me. I would shop, but only buy something because it was "*such a screamin' deal!*" The problem was that I didn't necessarily love the piece, but the price warranted a purchase. Ugh. This way of thinking—price-point shopping—led me to a closet full of crap, none of which I loved. I realized that the sale items were the most expensive items I owned. They were the biggest waste of money because I never wore them.

My general advice on items that cost more than you want to pay is to sleep on it. Do not purchase it right then and there. Give yourself a day to consider how much you really like the fit, color, and style. If you are still longing for that expensive item, then go get it.

I shop for items that fit my unique style and I save to purchase them. The latest item on my list is a pair of shoes for $300. When I have saved my pretty pennies, I'm going to buy them, wear them, and love them more because they hold value for me. I know that a good pair of shoes is worth every cent. After I've worn them out and it's time to let them go, I will thank the shoes for coming into my life and serving their purpose. Then I will release them to a donation center, no questions asked, even though they were $300. By shopping in this way, I curate and create a unique, classy, and sassy wardrobe full of items I love that make me feel like a 10.

Another way to justify a spendy piece of clothing or jewelry is to divide the number of times you are going to wear it by the cost. As an example, if I buy a Michael Kors purse for $300, I ask myself if I'm going to use it at least 300 days out of the year. If yes, then the cost equates to $1 per day. If the answer is no, the key is to figure out how many days per wear I'm going to get out of the purse.

Let's say it's three months for a seasonal satchel, or 90 days. The cost is roughly $3.34 per day. Is the cost per wear worth it? Perhaps in this case, yes. But what about $400 for that Kate Spade dress you will wear only once to your company Christmas party? Again, consider the cost/benefit analysis. Is it worth it to you? Does it make you feel like a 10? Can you wear it more than once? Only *you* can answer these questions. Make sure you sleep on it to determine if it's worth your hard-earned money!

Seasonal Shopping

One way to curate a great wardrobe is to shop seasonally over the course of the year. Once a quarter, buy two or three new outfits, including shoes and accessories. Do not buy one-off pieces; shop for complete looks. Try to include something in color, such as a new bag, shoes, or a blouse. This will ensure an updated wardrobe that looks great on you and is right on trend. Using the Fashion Formula, as described below, shop with confidence when purchasing outfits throughout the year! Before you know it, you will have a closet you love, full of updated pieces that look great on you.

PUTTING OUTFITS TOGETHER—THE FASHION FORMULA

The Fashion Formula is a four-step process. To feel your best, use this guide for getting dressed. This formula is used to put an outfit together. It's useful and makes sense. Hang the formula in your closet and use it when you are in a rut. Take it with you when you go shopping so that you stop the habit of buying the same thing over and over. I use this with my clients when we shop, as well as when we are creating outfits with the clothes they already have. It's easy to spot a deficiency in your closet if any one of the four sections in the formula are not in abundance.

One Basic: a dark wash jean, pencil skirt, dress, basic top

+

One Interest Piece: something of color, pattern, texture, shine

+

One Completer Piece: jacket, blazer, cardigan, belt, scarf

+

Accessories: earring, necklace, shoes, bag

=

One well-dressed hot-to-trot maven!

Wear Color Where It Counts

I love using color in my wardrobe. Playing with color such as a new lipstick, a fun accessory (think statement necklace or ring), or a shoe is a great way to appear as if you have style.

It's a good idea to discover the colors that look the best on you. By doing a color wheel analysis, I can determine a person's power colors, including their core body colors as well as the colors that look best on them. Do you know if you look better in a stark black, or is a deep charcoal better suited for your skin tone? Perhaps it's neither, and a deep chocolate is more appropriate. It is all very custom and based on an individual's eye color, hair color, skin tone, and the whites of their eyes and teeth. These vary greatly from human to human.

Color = Confidence

People who wear color project a level of quiet confidence. Even if you tend to wear a mostly black palette, confidence is shown when you punch up your outfit with a chunky colorful necklace, or bright pink lips. Some clients choose to incorporate color into their hair, on their nails, or with their shoes. Without saying a word, you are able to project confidence by using color.

One way to incorporate color is to wear lipstick. It's been around for thousands of years, and is a great way to show confidence. I suggest getting two colors that suit your skin tone: a red and a pink. Wearing a cooler blue-red or more of a warm orangey-red is determined by having your color palette done. The same warm/cool rules apply with pinks. Lipstick is a great way to brighten your face. If you had a long night, and the bags under your eyes are unbearable, a quick fashion tip is to put on a fantastic shade of lipstick and a statement earring. It creates a distraction, if you will, and nobody will even notice those tired eyes.

STRATEGIC COLOR ON YOUR BODY

It is important to use color in the right places and remember to consider your body shape. So here is the tip: if you carry your weight in your hips and thighs/legs, wear color in your blouse. It will draw the eye upwards and create balance with your unique shape. If you are heavier on top (could be a large chest, or broad shoulders) then wear a colored pair of slacks, jeans, or shoes. It will draw the eye towards your best features! I carry my weight in my butt, hips, and thighs. I often wear solid-color blouses in bright shades of pink, blue, and red. It minimizes the awareness I have (and what others see) of my "problem area" and helps to create some balance.

Emphasize your best feature with color. Do you have great legs? Buy a stunning pair of slacks in something other than black. Do you have a curvy body, with a small waist? Use a fun, colorful belt in the smallest part of your torso to cinch your blouse. Do you have large breasts that you always try to hide? Instead, opt for a fitted blouse that has a colorful pattern, which can be more slimming than a solid, loose-fitting shirt.

Do Yourself a Favor: Don't Force Color

As a stylist, it can be hard to own up to my own fashion faux-pas, but I have definitely had my fair share. One of the worst, I'm about to share with you. The lesson is when it comes to skin tone, embrace what you have.

It was the summer of 2008, and my cousin was getting married. The wedding was in Spokane, Washington, which can be really dry and hot in the summer. In my twenties at the time and single, I knew weddings were a great place to meet a mate.

So, I bought a beautiful blue, sleeveless, mid-thigh-length dress with a deep V in the back and front. The only problem is that the dress showed some skin, and I'm very fair. The blinding power of my white skin is not that flattering. I've been called "colorless" on more than one occasion, to give you an idea.

Lucky for me, I had a tall, blonde, beautiful coworker who told me all about spray tanning. So I made an appointment at the local shop near my house. They talked me into buying a package of three sessions, so I did. I was told to put the 'barrier cream' all over my body, especially my hands, knees, ankles...basically anywhere that can be really dry. Then, get undressed, put my hair in a net and step into the chamber. I was told the spray that came out of the machine was all aloe-based and I could breathe easy. It would not hurt me if inhaled.

So, I got undressed, put on the hair net, stepped into the chamber, closed the door and pushed the "start" button.

The spray came out with the force of a fire engine hose, moving up and down to evenly distribute my body with the dye. I freaked out. I didn't yell, scream, or jump out of the chamber. I froze and I tinkled. It wasn't a lot, just a couple of tense, freak-out drops. As soon as it happened, I knew that it would leave a streak. The few drops ran down the inside of my right leg taking all the dye with it. As the drops swirled around my ankle, I knew this was not going to be a good look.

The next day, I looked like an orange Oompa Loompa, but the worst part was down the inside of my right leg was a bare white streak where the dye didn't set. What had happened inside the tanning booth was obvious, however, I wore the dress anyway.

The moral of the story is to embrace your skin tone, whatever shade you are. Embrace it and enhance it by wearing the right color of clothes, not by adjusting the natural tones of your skin. Wear color where it counts with clothes, makeup, and accessories.

A STRESS-FREE SYSTEM FOR GETTING DRESSED

"My wife has only two complaints," said a husband. "One is that her closet isn't big enough, and the second is that she never has anything to wear."

One complaint I always hear from my clients is that they can't ever figure out what to wear in the morning. They stare at their closet, full of clothes, and then try on a million things before deciding on something that will "have to do." Meanwhile, twenty-five minutes has passed and massive frustration has ensued.

The 10-Minute Rule

I challenge my clients to implement this rule: set your timer for 10 minutes the night before, and choose your outfit, complete with accessories and shoes. If you have children, it's important that they also choose what they are going to wear the night before. Put it all on one hanger, with accessories and shoes nearby. (There is nothing worse than a child's missing shoe in the morning, as you're trying to pile everyone in the car.)

Don't second guess your choice the next morning. In other words, ignore the "I don't feel like wearing it" resistance that may pop up. Just do it. You had every confidence in the outfit you chose last night. Stick to your decision. Don't waste your precious morning time trying to figure out an outfit when you did it the night before. Adhere to the 10-minute outfit rule, and once you are in the habit, you won't ever look back.

I have one client who is an attorney and professor of law at the University of Washington. She does this every Sunday. While her husband watches the kids for thirty minutes, she prepares her five outfits for the workweek. Preparation is huge in reducing stress.

Need convincing? Think about the last trip you took. It's super easy to get dressed in the morning on vacation, because you have pre-selected your outfits. They are sitting in your suitcase, just waiting to be put on! Try the 10-minute outfit rule, or the half-hour Sunday rule for a month. Once it's habit, you will not struggle with what to wear in the morning.

ONE CLIENT'S JOURNEY

I want to leave you with a story that my client, Ingrid, wrote. I did not know she was chronicling her journey working with me, but when she shared it with me, it opened my eyes to how people may feel working with a stylist, which can be very intimidating. Written in her voice, I adore her honesty:

Closet Cleanse—Ingrid's Story

I had a range of unexpected emotions when Wendy came over for my closet cleanse. I was nervous, self-conscious, surprised, reassured, and excited.

What would Wendy think of my clothes and of my sense of style (or in my mind, lack of style)? I found that I was explaining every piece of clothing that I wore and why I only wore "these pants" with "this shirt" because otherwise, the undesirable parts of my body would show and I would feel uncomfortable. It actually surprised me how self-conscious I was about all of my clothes and how they looked on my body. It's one thing to get dressed in the morning and see the clothes on yourself and how they fit. It's another for an outsider to see it, especially if you aren't entirely comfortable with your body and you're always working to cover it up.

After we went through my closet, Wendy took an inventory of items I needed and also pointed out the clothes I had that she felt we could work with. I was surprised and delighted to find that I actually did have a lot of cute things to wear (mainly tops); I just needed to find pants or skirts to complete the outfits. We talked about what I needed and the potential outfits we could create and at that point, I was excited for the possibilities. I took a few months to save up and then we made an appointment to go shopping with $500. I was nervous as I was saving up and kept wondering, "What if we can't find many clothes that fit me? What if I'm not able to get many items for my budgeted amount? What if Wendy recommends clothes I didn't like and I have to say no?"

Second Appointment—Shopping

The goal of the shopping expedition was to enhance my professional wardrobe. Five hundred dollars and an afternoon after work shopping with Wendy resulted in three pairs of pants, four blouses, one belt, one blazer, one pair of stockings, and one black dress for work. I normally shop at Ross or Target and try to find the best deals possible. Often, I sacrifice look for affordability. This time, I reminded myself of Wendy's advice and kept considering this question: It may be an item that costs more than I would normally spend, but am I going to wear it enough times for it to be well worth the cost?

We went to my favorite store first: Banana Republic. We stuck to the sale racks and ended up finding three blouses, a belt and a black dress. Then, we moved on to Nordstrom Rack. In all honesty, I dread Nordstrom Rack because it's overwhelming for me to shop there. But, it wasn't so hard with Wendy's help. We filled up a cart full of clothes and spent about an hour trying them on in different combinations. End result: a very comfortable and flattering pair of work pants, a beautiful designer blouse in colors I don't normally wear. To my surprise, though, the shades of green and blue made my hair and eyes pop. I also bought an awesome blazer that has a style/cut that really complements my body shape. The third and last place we went was Macy's where I walked away with two more pairs of pants and a cute pair of knit stockings.

I learned two things from this shopping experience: 1) Be flexible and open minded, and 2) when trying on clothes, try them on in multiple ways. It surprised me how different clothes look when doing those two simple things.

In all honesty, the experiences I've had so far with Wendy have changed me. I'm feeling good about what I'm wearing and that, in turn, has increased my confidence in myself. I'm starting to wear more color and I'm learning to add more accessories to what I'm wearing to create that "put-together" look for myself. I've realized I'm worth it and that feels amazing!"

THAT'S A WRAP...

In Ingrid's story, I think we all find parts we can relate to. She is brutally honest about her insecurities in regard to her body, clothing choices, and most of all, working with a stylist.

As a full-time stylist, I know that everyone has experiences like this (even stylists ourselves). I would be amiss to tell you that I don't feel frumpy on some days. Not every day is a "slam dunk." Expecting perfection from yourself as you up-level your confidence is a sure-fire way to fail and not find it. Start out small. Set goals over the next 365 days that are reasonable and fun. And by all means, if you need help, seek it out. If fashion is not your zone of genius, find someone who does it well and learn what you can from them. Often, it's worth the money to hire expert help.

Remember, ask yourself what you want to accomplish in the next 365 days in regard to how you want to present yourself to the world. Find clarity and dive into your closet head first. By cleaning out your closet, you are making room for something new and fantastic in your life. Focus on what you want to invite in, and then start the cleaning-out process to bring it closer to you. Over the course of the next 365 days you will find your foundation of carefully curated clothing items will steadily grow, as will your confidence.

"Wendy helped me break through some fashion 'rules' or 'shackles' about what larger women should not wear and helped my journey for self-acceptance."
—Darla Pritchard (Emerald)

Wendy Petersen
DRES System Certified Personal Stylist

Bellevue, Washington
stylebywendy@gmail.com
dressystem.com

Wendy Petersen is the successful business owner of Style By Wendy, located in Seattle, Washington. As a Certified Personal Stylist, she uses her knowledge from the DRES System and her experience working at Nordstrom to help men and women who feel frumpy find more confidence in their closets. You can find Wendy and her team at expos, many networking events, and in corporate America giving presentations at offices in the form of lunch-n-learn gatherings.

She first attended Cottey College, an all-women's college located in Nevada, Missouri. From there, Wendy earned her B.S. in Biological Science from Washington State University. After WSU, she went to Middleburg College in Vermont to continue studying French. After graduating college, she worked in corporate America for giants such as Xerox, Nordstrom, and Alliant before striking out on her own. Wendy also holds her producer license to sell insurance in the state of Washington.

Now that Wendy owns her own company, she has never looked back. The rewarding experience of helping clients find their confidence keeps her going every day. Wendy wants to be known for her customer service and all things associated with closets. She would like to thank her clients for the wonderful support and referrals, as well as her husband who gave her the push she needed to jump off the deep-end and start a business.

Wendy is very active in a group called Philanthropic Educational Organization (PEO). Their charter is to educate women across the globe by providing money through scholarships and loans to attend school. She has been a member for twelve years, holding different positions. She most recently held a state position for three years, and prior to that a district position for two years. Wendy and her family volunteer one weekend every summer at Camp Prime Time, a summer camp for mentally and physically disabled children and their families. Wendy enjoys hanging out with her husband and large family, going for walks, and reading business books. She loves ceviche, an ice-cold beer, the sun, and travelling. Her biggest weakness is a tall, skinny vanilla latte.

HOW TO FIND IMAGE CONFIDENCE

"I've got this figure of mine that looks impossible in off-the-rack clothes. If the length's right, then the top swims on me. It's very discouraging to see yourself looking practically malformed. I loathe trying on clothes."

—Audrey Hepburn

THE DRES DIFFERENCE

Sure there are other styling services available, but DRES is one of a kind. Not only do we have a scientific process of determining what makes you look your best and amazing styling tools, we also have the nicest stylists around. We share a joint vision for empowering people to become their personal best and we go beyond the clothing to see the greatness in each individual.

DRES SYSTEM CONSULTING

The DRES System offers personal style education for improved confidence and clarity. Let us help you curate your clothing collection to create the wardrobe of your dreams. At dressystem.com, we offer a network of personal stylists to help everyone feel and look confident.

From in-home consultations to personal shopping, there is nothing like the warmth of working with a friendly Personal Stylist who cares for you and will keep you looking your best. To discover the best services for you, schedule a free introductory call with one of our Personal Stylists or contact us for help in finding a DRES System Certified Personal Stylist in your area.

DRES WORKSHOPS

Many of our stylists offer workshops to inspire your style. We host these at a variety of locations and partner with local businesses to bring you fresh new experiences at each session. Here you get the benefit of meeting and greeting a stylist prior to a one-on-one appointment. Look for dates on our website.

HOW DRES CONSULTING WORKS

Empowering Three-Step Consulting Process

Our process has essential steps to provide you with the best service possible. STEP 1) Profile, STEP 2) Organize, STEP 3) Shop, is our three-step consulting process. With a smooth flow, the consulting process equips you with the information, tools, and support you need to have a balanced wardrobe that brings out your brilliance. Below is our full menu of services.

Profile

It all starts with the profile. The only way to build the ultimate wardrobe is by starting with the right foundation. Here, we help to define your fashion style, color range, and your body's unique proportions. We assess your lifestyle and clothing needs. This service includes our DRES Style Guide, which is a style book personalized just for you. A custom color palette can be added to this service for your ultimate 42 colors.

"It's not the money that makes you well dressed,
it's understanding."

—Christian Dior

Color Assessment

We'll bring out your brilliance by defining your 42 Ultimate Colors out of over five hundred! We use our exclusive DRES System colors to provide a detailed assessment of your individual coloring, and create a personalized Color Palette.

Organize

Nothing can be purchased before we know what you already have. We work with you to edit your wardrobe, narrowing it down to your best pieces. Through this process and the profile, we advise you on your missing pieces with a shopping list to round out your wardrobe. Your closet is now well-organized, sorted into categories, and looking like a personal boutique.

"True elegance consists not in having a closet bursting with clothes, but rather in having a few well-chosen numbers in which one feels totally at ease."

—Coco Chanel

Shop

Now that we have a shopping list, we can help you track down the best items that fit your profile. Personal shopping can be done for you and delivered to you, or we can guide you on a private shopping experience.

Outfit Styling

Your stylist will show you how to coordinate and document outfits from your wardrobe. You'll receive a beautiful photo catalog to easily reference your best looks.

Face Styling

We'll determine your facial proportions and discuss the best way to dress your face to complement your features. Discover the best hairstyles, glasses, accessories, and makeup for your face shape, and proportions.

"Women usually love what they buy, yet hate two-thirds of what is in their closets."

—Mignon McLaughlin

Wardrobe Update

Refresh your wardrobe before each new season by clearing out the old and bringing in the new. Your stylist will work with you to incorporate new trends that are appropriate for you, help you get organized, and create new outfits for the season ahead.

Special Occasions

Need help finding the perfect outfit for a wedding, black-tie event, business meeting, or reunion? Maybe you need help packing for your whole trip. We can help you put together a complete outfit that is perfect so you can look and feel your best.

Shopping Tours

Are you traveling to a new city on business or pleasure? If you have a few hours, contact one of our DRES System Certified Stylists to put together a personalized tour. We'll save you time by taking you directly to the best boutiques in the city that are just your style.

DRES TOOLS

DRES Tools are exclusively available through our DRES System Certified Personal Stylists. They are included during private in-home consulting appointments and designed to bring clarity to your wardrobe selections.

StyleGuides

The personalized StyleGuide is a book that's customized for you by your DRES Stylist. It takes the stress out of shopping and helps you stay focused on what styles works best for you. This product is included in the profile appointment.

Color Palette

Just like a custom-made painting, the personalized color palette holds fabric swatches of your 42 Ultimate Colors narrowed down from over five hundred possibilities. This product is included in the color assessment appointment.

JOIN US

We are always looking for talented people in all cities. In order to join our team of Personal Stylists and become certified in our DRES System, you must first complete our online comprehensive training program, complete fieldwork, and pass our exam. Some of our Personal Stylists are just starting out, others have previous experience and bring with them extended knowledge in a variety of areas. Each Stylist in our national network is an independent business owner.

The DRES Personal Stylist training and certification course is offered through a comprehensive online program. The high-quality video training shows live client consultations and models our consulting method. We provide you with everything needed to start a consulting business, including team meetings and ongoing support. Certification can be completed.

BEYOND DRES

Through the years I have worked with a lot of women and have been moved by the deep emotions that come to the surface with this process. Feeling good about yourself is deeply important to women. When they feel for the first time they can have control over their image, it is empowering. I have seen tears of joy (with lots of hugs) after a successful transformation through the DRES System. I have also seen women cry while telling me they have never been told they were, or felt, beautiful.

I love the calls I get after working with clients who are thrilled that they are getting compliments on their new looks. One client was so surprised that even strangers were stopping her on the street to compliment her new outfit. Even though it is nice to get compliments, DRES Stylists know that there are lasting positive effects on someone's confidence that go beyond dressing. When most people see our clients newfound confidence they think it's because of their new style; however, their confidence lies in believing in their inner beauty. That is why our Personal Stylists go beyond DRES.

WHAT PEOPLE SAY

"I have gotten compliments from three different people today. This did not happen before working with you!"

—Sara Yao (Diamond)

"I like that the DRES System has simplified terminology so I did not have to figure out if the clothes were meant for me."

—Jody Hurd (Emerald)

"The DRES System wardrobe makeover was a wonderful experience for me. At first, I was a little nervous about inviting someone into my house to do an in-depth look at my body shape and my clothes. But once we began, the whole thing was easy and comfortable. The change in my confidence has been apparent to my family, friends, and co-workers, and I encourage every woman to have an honest, helpful guide who can show you how to look beautiful and dress well, no matter what your shape or size. Thank you DRES System."

—Erica Gaddis (Sapphire)

"Although I had a closet full of clothes, I still always found myself standing there overwhelmed and frustrated that I could never find anything to wear! The DRES System helped me better understand what styles and colors best complement me. I realize now that I do not have to hide behind "maternity-style" shirts anymore; I feel more confident wearing clothes that best accentuate my body shape. The DRES System is a very useful guide and has helped make shopping for clothes a more enjoyable experience."

—Julie Raupp (Ruby)

"They helped me 'think outside the box' and guided me toward pieces I may not have ever chosen on my own. Their experienced eyes saved me a lot of time. I'm so glad I did this! I know I learned how to make better choices and spend my money wisely for future purchases."

—Karen Herrema (Emerald)

ACKNOWLEDGEMENTS

There is only so much you can accomplish alone. Together we are unstoppable. Pulling together a book takes a lot more than the efforts of one person—it takes a team. Publishing a book takes designers, layout artists, writers, editors, proofreaders, managers, and lots of persistence.

I am so grateful to the Beyond DRES team who worked on this book. Most of all, I really could not have done this without the editors, layout artist, and proofreaders who worked diligently on this project.

To my co-authors, this has been a journey for each of us and when you go through a journey with challenges and triumphs it brings you closer together. I will always have a special bond with these ladies who made this book what it is today—a piece of all of our hearts united as one in an effort to make the world a little brighter.

The dedication of my leadership team warms my heart. Lisa Fischer, our Director of Education, has been such a joy to work with and I have had the privilege to watch her bloom, both as an individual and a stylist through the years. Lori Goddard-Weed, our Director of Events, has been integral in bringing our team together to host beautiful gatherings that spread insights from our DRES team.

I could not have done it without all of you. Hugs!

With warm regards,
Margaret Spencer

You're a gem; shine on!